A Foreign Country

Peter Ellison

A Foreign Country

*Exploring prose and
poetry from the past*

Peter Ellison

Hodder & Stoughton
LONDON SYDNEY AUCKLAND

Acknowledgments

The publishers would like to thank the following for giving permission to reproduce copyright photographic material in this book:

Cover, 'The Wanderer in a Sea of Fog' by Caspar David Friedrich/Hamburger Kunsthalle; p5, The Bridgeman Art Library/Whitford and Hughes, London; p9, Reproduced by kind permission of MacConnal-Mason Gallery, London; p10, Asha Lodh; p14, By courtesy of the Board of Trustees of the Victoria and Albert Museum; p29, The Illustrated London News Picture Library; p32/34, By courtesy of the Board of Trustees of the Victoria and Albert Museum; p41, 'The Hireling Shepherd' by William Holman Hunt, 1851/Manchester City Art Galleries ©; p45, By permission of the Trustees of the Tate Gallery; p52, The Bridgeman Art Library/City of Bristol Museum and Art Gallery; p63, The Mansell Collection; p78, Mary Evans Picture Library; p84, Peter Newark's Western Americana; p93, The Bridgeman Art Library/Pushkin Museum, Moscow; p95, The Imperial War Museum; p98, Peter Newark's Western Americana; p105, Mary Evans Picture Library; p109, Birmingham Museums and Art Gallery; p113/120, Peter Newark's Western Americana; p123, Punch Publications Ltd; p133, Barnaby's Picture Library; p136, The Illustrated London News Picture Library; p139, UPI/Bettmann Newsphotos; p143, 'Vanitas' by Harmen Steenwijck, c1656/Municipal Museum 'De Lakenhal', Leiden/The Netherlands; p144, The Bridgeman Art Library/Josef Mensing Gallery, Hamm-Rhynern; p148, 'Geezah, The Sphinx and the Great Pyramid' by Francis Frith/The Royal Photographic Society, Bath; p151, 'Der Tod als Freund' by Richard Julius Jungtow, after Alfred Rethel/Staatliche Kunstsammlungen Dresden.

British Library Cataloguing in Publication Data

Ellison, Peter
  A foreign country.
  I. Title
  821

ISBN 0-340-55627-7

First published 1992

© 1992 Peter Ellison

Typeset by Keyset Composition, Colchester, Essex.
Printed in Great Britain for the educational publishing division of Hodder & Stoughton Ltd, Mill Road, Dunton Green, Sevenoaks, Kent by St Edmundsbury Press, Bury St Edmunds, Suffolk.

Contents

unit 1

Children

Over the centuries, our attitude towards children has changed many times; for example, in the sixteenth century they were seen as little adults, whereas they were regarded as angels in the Victorian period. This unit examines childhood (from infancy to adolescence) as poets or novelists have seen it.

Joy and sadness

The following five poems and one prose extract deal with the mixed emotions that children bring out in adults.

Infant Joy

I have no name
I am but two days old.—
What shall I call thee?
I happy am
Joy is my name,—
Sweet joy befall thee!

Pretty joy!
Sweet joy but two days old.
Sweet joy I call thee:
Thou dost smile.
I sing the while
Sweet joy befall thee.

William Blake (1757–1827)

Anecdote for Fathers

I have a boy of five years old;
His face is fair and fresh to see;
His limbs are cast in beauty's mould,
And dearly he loves me.

One morn we strolled on our dry walk,
Our quiet home all full in view,
And held such intermitted talk
As we are wont to do.

My thoughts on former pleasures ran;
I thought of Kilve's delightful shore,
Our pleasant home when spring began,
A long, long year before.

A day it was when I could bear
Some fond regrets to entertain;
With so much happiness to spare,
I could not feel a pain.

The green earth echoed to the feet
Of lambs that bounded through the glade,
From shade to sunshine, and as fleet
From sunshine back to shade.

Birds warbled round me – and each trace
Of inward sadness had its charm;
Kilve, thought I, was a favoured place,
And so is Liswyn farm.

My boy beside me tripped, so slim
And graceful in his rustic dress!
And, as we talked, I questioned him,
In very idleness.

'Now tell me, had you rather be,'
I said, and took him by the arm,
'On Kilve's smooth shore, by the green sea,
Or here at Liswyn Farm?'

In careless mood he looked at me,
While still I held him by the arm,
And said, 'At Kilve I'd rather be
Than here at Liswyn Farm.'

'Now, little Edward, say why so:
My little Edward, tell me why.'–
'I cannot tell, I do not know.'–
'Why, this is strange,' said I;

'For here are woods, hills smooth and warm:
There surely must some reason be
Why you would change sweet Liswyn farm
For Kilve by the green sea.'

At this my boy hung down his head,
He blushed with shame, nor made reply;
And three times to the child I said,
'Why, Edward, tell me why?'

His head he raised – there was in sight,
It caught his eye, he saw it plain –
Upon the house-top, glittering bright,
A broad and gilded vane.

Then did the boy his tongue unlock,
And eased his mind with this reply:
'At Kilve there was no weather-cock;
And that's the reason why.'

O dearest, dearest boy! my heart
For better lore would seldom yearn,
Could I but teach the hundredth part
Of what from thee I learn.

William Wordsworth (1770–1850)

4

Concerning Gargantua's Childhood

From his third to his fifth year Gargantua was brought up and disciplined in all necessary ways, such being his father's orders; and he spent that time in the same manner as the other little children of that country: that is to say in drinking, eating, and sleeping; in eating, sleeping, and drinking; in sleeping, drinking, and eating.

He was always rolling in the mud, dirtying his nose, scratching his face, and treading down his shoes; and often he gaped after flies, or ran joyfully after the butterflies of whom his father was the ruler. He pissed in his shoes, shat in his shirt, wiped his nose on his sleeve, snivelled into his soup, paddled about everywhere, drank out of his slipper, and usually rubbed his belly on a basket. He sharpened his teeth on a shoe, washed his hands in soup, combed his hair with a wine-bowl, sat between two stools with his arse on the ground, covered himself with a wet sack, drank while eating his soup, ate his biscuit without bread, bit as he laughed and laughed as he bit, often spat in the dish, blew a fat fart, pissed against the sun, ducked under water to avoid the rain, struck the iron while it was cold, had empty thoughts, put on airs, threw up his food or, as they said, flayed the fox, mumbled his prayers like a monkey, returned to his muttons, and turned the sows out to hay. He would beat the dog in front of the lion, put the cart before the oxen, scratch where he did not itch, draw the worms from his nose, grip so hard that he caught nothing, eat his white bread first, shoe the grasshoppers, and tickle himself to make himself laugh. He was a good guzzler in the kitchen, offered the gods straw for grain, sang *Magnificat* at matins and thought this the right time, ate cabbages and shat beet, could find the flies in his milk and pulled the legs off them, scrawled on paper, blotted parchment, got away by his heels, played ducks and drakes with his purse, reckoned without his host, beat the bushes and missed the birds, and took the clouds for brass frying-pans and bladders for lanterns. He would draw two loads from one sack, play the donkey to get the bran, use his fist for a mallet, take cranes at the first leap, think a coat of mail was made link by link, always look a gift horse in the mouth, ramble from cock to bull, put one ripe fruit between two green, make the best of a bad job, protect the moon from the wolves, hope to catch larks if the heavens fell, take a slice of whatever bread he was offered, care as little for the bald as for the shaven, and flay the fox every morning. His father's little dogs ate out of his dish, and he ate with them. He bit their ears and they scratched his nose; he blew at their rumps and they licked his lips.

François Rabelais (c. 1494–c. 1553)

Letty's Globe

When Letty had scarce pass'd her third glad year,
And her young, artless words began to flow,
One day we gave the child a colour'd sphere
Of the wide earth, that she might mark and know,
By tint and outline, all its sea and land.
She patted all the world; old empires peep'd
Between her baby fingers; her soft hand
Was welcome at all frontiers. How she leap'd,
And laugh'd, and prattled in her world-wide bliss;
But when we turned her sweet unlearned eye
On our own isle, she raised a joyous cry,
'Oh! yes, I see it, Letty's home is there!'
And, while she hid all England with a kiss,
Bright over Europe fell her golden hair.

Charles Tennyson Turner (1808–1879)

Epitaph on her Son H. P. at St Syth's Church, where her body also lies interred

What on earth deserves our trust?
Youth and beauty both are dust.
Long we gathering are with pain,
What one moment calls again.
Seven years' childless marriage past,
A son, a son is born at last:
So exactly limbed and fair,
Full of good spirits, mien, and air,
As a long life promised,
Yet, in less than six weeks dead.
Too promising, too great a mind
In so small room to be confined:
Therefore, as fit in Heav'n to dwell,
He quickly broke the prison shell.
So the subtle alchemist
Can't with Hermes' seal resist
The powerful spirit's subtler flight,
But 'twill bid him long good night:
And so the sun, if it arise
Half so glorious as his eyes,
Like this infant, takes a shroud,
Buried in a morning cloud.

Katherine Philips (1631–1664)

On my First Sonne

Farewell, thou child of my right hand, and joy;
   My sinne was too much hope of thee, lov'd boy,
Seven yeeres tho'wert lent to me, and I thee pay,
   Exacted by thy fate, on the just day.
O, could I loose all father, now. For why
   Will man lament the state he should envie?
To have so soone scap'd worlds, and fleshes rage,
   And, if no other miserie, yet age?
Rest in soft peace, and, ask'd, say here doth lye
   BEN. JONSON his best piece of *poetrie*.
For whose sake, hence-forth, all his vowes be such,
   As what he loves may never like too much.

Ben Jonson (1573–1637)

Ideas for discussion

■ Read the first four pieces carefully again. How do they compare with your own experience of the way very young children behave and the way that adults react to them?

■ 'Infant Joy' and 'Anecdote for Fathers' are dialogues between parents and children. In the first poem, the baby is only two days old and yet Blake has it speak. How can it communicate with its parent?

In the second poem, the child speaks reluctantly, questioned by his father. His answers seem irrational and random, and yet the poet says that he has learned from this exchange. What could he possibly have learned? How realistic do you find these two conversations?

■ 'Concerning Gargantua's Childhood' and 'Letty's Globe' paint very different pictures of childhood. How true do you find these pictures? Do you think Turner would have written the same poem about a boy or that Rabelais would have described a girl's childhood in these terms?

■ 'Epitaph on her son H. P.' and 'On my First Sonne' were both written after the death of children.

Read both poems carefully. How do the poets attempt to deal with their grief? What arguments do they use to dull the pain of loss?

Suggestions for writing

1 Write an essay entitled 'Views of Childhood' in which you discuss each of the poems in detail and compare the ways in which they convey the behaviour of children and the feelings of parents.

2 Write a modern version of 'Gargantua's Childhood' by listing some of the things that a modern child might do or think up to the age of three or four (for instance, he or she might think that people live inside the TV).

3 Write a conversation between a five year old and his or her father or mother. You could, like Wordsworth, have the parent questioning the child or you could have it the other way round with the child asking the kind of difficult question that young children ask ('Why are you so ugly?' 'What are those dogs doing?'). Try to make it as realistic as possible.

Because a five year old is likely to have only short conversations, you will need to concentrate on the child's expression and body language as well as the actual words spoken. You may like to write a series of conversations that take place over the course of a day or two.

Growing up

This section deals with the delight and pain of growing up, culminating in the adolescent's desire for independence. Throughout the centuries the various stages of growing up have taken place at different ages. Smollett, writing in the eighteenth century, for instance, has his hero, Roderick Random, go to university at fourteen, but Lupin Pooter from the Victorian *Diary of a Nobody* does not rebel against his parents until he is twenty.

• Eppie in the Coal-hole •

George Eliot (real name Mary Ann Evans) wrote *Silas Marner* in 1860. It is the tale of a weaver who is forced to move away from home to live alone in the village of Raveloe. He manages to save up a large amount of gold, but is horrified when this is stolen from him. Not long afterwards, however, it seems that his gold is returned in the form of a golden-haired little girl who is abandoned on his doorstep. Through the love of this little girl, Eppie, he rebuilds his life.

In this extract, he finds that the angelic little girl has become rather more independent than he would like.

[. . .]by the time Eppie was three years old, she developed a fine capacity for mischief, and for devising ingenious ways of being troublesome, which found much exercise, not only for Silas's patience, but for his watchfulness and penetration. Sorely was poor Silas puzzled on such occasions by the incompatible demands of love. Dolly Winthrop told him that punishment was good for Eppie, and that, as for rearing a child without making it tingle a little in soft and safe places now and then, it was not to be done.

'To be sure, there's another thing you might do, Master Marner,' added Dolly, meditatively: 'you might shut her up once i' the coal-hole. That was what I did wi' Aaron; for I was that silly wi' the youngest lad, as I could never bear to smack him. Not as I could find i' my heart to let him stay i' the coal-hole more nor a minute, but it was enough to colly* him all over, so as he must be new washed and dressed, and it was as good as a rod to him – that was. But I put it upo' your conscience, Master Marner, as there's one of 'em you must choose – ayther smacking or the coal-hole – else she'll get so masterful, there'll be no holding her.'

Silas was impressed with the melancholy truth of this last remark; but his force of mind failed before the only two penal methods open to him, not only because it was painful to him to hurt Eppie, but because he trembled at a moment's contention with her, lest she should love him the less for it. Let even an affectionate Goliath get himself tied to a smaller tender thing, dreading to hurt it by pulling, and dreading still more to snap the cord, and which of the two, pray, will be master? It was clear that Eppie, with her short toddling steps, must lead father Silas a

*dirty

pretty dance on any fine morning when circumstances favoured mischief.

For example. He had wisely chosen a broad strip of linen as a means of fastening her to his loom when he was busy: it made a broad belt round her waist, and was long enough to allow of her reaching the truckle-bed and sitting down on it, but not long enough for her to attempt any dangerous climbing. One bright summer's morning Silas had been more engrossed than usual in 'setting up' a new piece of work, an occasion on which his scissors were in requisition. These scissors, owing to an especial warning of Dolly's, had been kept carefully out of Eppie's reach; but the click of them had had a peculiar attraction for her ear, and, watching the results of that click, she had derived the philosophic lesson that the same cause would produce the same effect. Silas had seated himself in his loom, and the noise of weaving had begun; but he had left his scissors on a ledge which Eppie's arm was long enough to reach; and now, like a small mouse, watching her opportunity, she stole quietly from her corner, secured the scissors, and toddled to the bed again, setting up her back as a mode of concealing the fact. She had a distinct intention as to the use of the scissors; and having cut the linen strip in a jagged but effectual manner, in two moments she had run out at the open door where the sunshine was inviting her, while poor Silas believed her to be a better child than usual. It was not until he happened to need his scissors that the terrible fact burst upon him: Eppie had run out by herself – had perhaps fallen into the Stone-pit. Silas, shaken by the worst fear that could have befallen him, rushed out, calling 'Eppie!' and ran eagerly about the unenclosed space, exploring the dry cavities into which she might have fallen, and then gazing with questioning dread at the smooth red surface of the water. The cold drops stood on his brow. How long had she been out? There was one hope – that she had crept through the stile and got into the fields, where he habitually took her to stroll. But the grass was high in the meadow, and there was no descrying her, if she were there, except by a close search that would be a trespass on Mr Osgood's crop. Still, that misdemeanour must be committed; and poor Silas, after peering all round the hedgerows, traversed the grass, beginning with perturbed vision to see Eppie behind every group of red sorrel, and to see her moving always farther off as he approached. The meadow was searched in vain; and he got over the stile into the next field, looking with dying hope towards a small pond which was now reduced to its summer shallowness, so as to leave a wide margin of good adhesive mud.

Here, however, sat Eppie, discoursing cheerfully to her own small boot, which she was using as a bucket to convey the water into a deep hoof-mark, while her little naked foot was planted comfortably on a cushion of olive-green mud. A red-headed calf was observing her with alarmed doubt through the opposite hedge.

Here was clearly a case of aberration in a christened child which demanded severe treatment; but Silas, overcome with convulsive joy at finding his treasure again, could do nothing but snatch her up, and cover her with half-sobbing kisses. It was not until he had carried her home, and had begun to think of the necessary washing, that he recollected the need that he should punish Eppie, and 'make her remember'. The idea that she might run away again and come to harm, gave him unusual resolution, and for the first time he determined to try the coal-hole – a small closet near the hearth.

'Naughty, naughty Eppie,' he suddenly began, holding her on his knee, and pointing to her muddy feet and clothes – 'naughty to cut with the scissors and run away. Eppie must go into the coal-hole for being naughty. Daddy must put her in the coal-hole.'

He half-expected that this would be shock enough, and that Eppie would begin to cry. But instead of that, she began to shake herself on his knee, as if the proposition opened a pleasing novelty. Seeing that he must proceed to extremities, he put her into the coal-hole, and held the door closed, with a trembling sense that he was using a strong measure. For a moment there was silence, but then came a little cry, 'Opy, opy!' and Silas let her out again, saying, 'Now Eppie 'ull never be naughty again, else she must go into the coal-hole – a black naughty place.'

The weaving must stand still a long while this morning, for now Eppie must be washed, and have clean clothes on; but it was to be hoped that this punishment would have a lasting effect, and save time in future – though, perhaps, it would have been better if Eppie had cried more.

In half an hour she was clean again, and Silas having turned his back to see what he could do with the linen band, threw it down again, with the reflection that Eppie would be good without fastening for the rest of the morning. He turned round again, and was going to place her in her little chair near the loom, when she peeped out at him with black face and hands again, and said, 'Eppie in de toal-hole!'.

George Eliot (1819–1880)

17

Ideas for discussion

- How realistic is this portrayal of a toddler? Compare it with your own experience of three year olds.

- Silas reacts to the child's disappearance with rising panic. How does Eliot convey his state of mind?

- Silas rejects the idea of smacking Eppie but his alternative punishment fails dismally. How do you feel about the corporal punishment of children? If you had a child, what form of punishment, if any, would you choose?

Suggestions for writing

1 How do modern parents attempt to discipline toddlers? Write your own story in which a mother or father deals with a naughty toddler. You could try to make it humorous with, for example, the child running rings around the adult.

2 Write an essay in which you discuss your views on the disciplining of young children.

• Idolatry •

Edmund Gosse was born into a family of Plymouth Brethren, an extreme Christian sect, and was dedicated at birth to 'the service of the Lord'. In 1907 he published his autobiography, *Father and Son*, anonymously, and it was immediately praised for its unmasking of Victorian hypocrisy.

In this extract, Edmund discovers that his father does not know all of God's ways.

It was about the date of my sixth birthday that I did something very naughty, some act of direct disobedience, for which my Father, after a solemn sermon, chastised me, sacrificially, by giving me several cuts with a cane. This action was justified, as everything he did was justified, by reference to Scripture – 'Spare the rod and spoil the child'. I suppose that there are some children, of a sullen and lymphatic temperament, who are smartened up and made more wide-awake by a whipping. It is largely a matter of convention, the exercise being endured (I am told) with pride by the infants of our aristocracy, but not tolerated by the lower classes. I am afraid that I proved my inherent vulgarity by being made, not contrite or humble, but furiously angry by this caning. I cannot account for the flame of rage which it awakened in my bosom. My dear, excellent Father had beaten me, not very severely, without ill-temper, and with the most genuine desire to improve me. But he was not well-advised especially so far as the 'dedication to the Lord's service' was concerned. This name 'dedication' had ministered to my vanity, and there are some natures which are not improved by being humiliated. I have to confess with shame that I went about the house for some days with a murderous hatred of my Father locked within my bosom. He did not suspect that the chastisement had not been wholly efficacious, and he bore me no malice; so that after a while, I forgot and thus forgave him. But I do not regard physical punishment as a wise element in the education of proud and sensitive children.

My theological misdeeds culminated, however, in an act so puerile and preposterous that I should not venture to record it if it did not throw some glimmering of light on the subject which I have proposed to myself in writing these pages. My mind continued to dwell on the mysterious question of prayer. It puzzled me greatly to know why, if we were God's children, and if he was watching over us by night and day, we might not supplicate for toys and sweets and smart clothes as well as for the conversion of the heathen. Just at this juncture, we had a special service at the Room, at which our attention was particularly called to what we always spoke of as 'the field of missionary labour'. The East was represented among 'the saints' by an excellent Irish peer, who had, in his early youth, converted and married a lady of colour; this Asiatic shared in our Sunday morning meetings, and was an object of helpless terror to me; I shrank from her amiable caresses, and vaguely identified her with a personage much spoken of in our family circle, the 'Personal Devil'.

All these matters drew my thoughts to the subject of idolatry, which was severely censured at the missionary meeting. I cross-examined my Father very closely as to the nature of this sin, and pinned him down to the categorical statement that idolatry consisted in praying to any one or anything but God himself. Wood and stone, in the words of the hymn, were peculiarly liable to be bowed down to by the heathen in their blindness. I pressed my Father further on this subject, and he assured me that God would be very angry, and would signify His anger, if anyone, in a Christian country, bowed down to wood and stone. I cannot recall why I was so pertinacious on this subject, but I remember that my Father became a little restive under my cross-examination. I determined, however, to test the matter for myself, and one morning, when both my parents were safely out of the house, I prepared for the great act of heresy. I was in the morning-room on the ground-floor, where, with much labour, I hoisted a small chair on to the table close to the window. My heart was now beating as if it would leap out of my side, but I pursued my experiment. I knelt down on the carpet in front of the table and looking up I said my daily prayer in a loud voice, only substituting the address 'O Chair!' for the habitual one.

Having carried this act of idolatry safely through, I waited to see what would happen. It was a fine day, and I gazed up at the slip of white sky above the houses opposite, and expected something to appear in it. God would certainly exhibit his anger in some terrible form, and would chastise my impious and wilful action. I was very much alarmed, but still more excited; I breathed the high, sharp air of defiance. But nothing happened; there was not a cloud in the sky, not an unusual sound in the street. Presently I was quite sure that nothing would happen. I had committed idolatry, flagrantly and deliberately, and God did not care.

The result of this ridiculous act was not to make me question the existence and power of God; those were forces which I did not dream of ignoring. But what it did was to lessen still further my confidence in my Father's knowledge of the Divine mind. My Father had said, positively, that if I worshipped a thing made of wood, God would manifest his anger. I had then worshipped a chair, made (or partly made) of wood, and God had made no sign whatever. My Father, therefore, was not really acquainted with the Divine practice in cases of idolatry. And with that, dismissing the subject, I dived again into the unplumbed depths of the *Penny Cyclopaedia*.

Edmund Gosse (1849–1928)

Ideas for discussion

- What do you think makes Edmund commit his act of idolatry?
- As a child, do you ever remember doing something that you knew to be wrong? Why did you do it? How did you feel?
- How do you think Edmund's attitude to his father is likely to change after this episode?

Suggestions for writing

Write your own story in which a child or young person defies the beliefs of his or her parents. Here are some ideas to help you:

- The child of Communist parents joins the Young Conservatives.

- The child of a religious family refuses to worship.

- The child of atheistic parents develops a religious faith.

- The child of vegetarian parents comes home eating a beefburger.

● The Little One ●

This is an extract from the French writer Colette's reminiscences of her childhood, *My Mother's House*. Although the passage is written in the third person, The Little One of the title is Colette herself.

And now all is silence in the garden. First one cat, then two more, stretch and yawn before extending a doubtful paw to test the gravel path, just as they do after a storm. They set off towards the house, and the Little One, having started to follow them, pauses: she does not feel worthy. She will wait until her normal pallor, like an inner dawn that celebrates the departure of evil demons, rises again into her hot cheeks still dark with over-excitement. She opens her wide mouth for a final shout, showing her recently cut eye-teeth. She opens her eyes to the full, wrinkles her forehead, give vent to a 'pouf' of exhaustion, and wipes her nose on the back of her hand.

A school pinafore envelops her like a sack from neck to knees, and her hair, after the fashion of poor children, is looped in two plaits behind her ears. What will become of her hands, clawed and scratched by cats and brambles, or of her feet laced into boots of light brown kid? There are days when they say that the Little One will be pretty later on. Today she is ugly, and feels upon her face the passing ugliness of her perspiration, the marks of dirty fingers on her cheek and, above all, the successive mimicries that have linked her with Jeanne, with Sandrine, with Aline, the daily dressmaker, with the chemist's wife and the postmaster's daughter. For the children had crowned the afternoon's sport with a long game of 'What shall we be when we're grown up?'

'When I'm grown up, I shall . . .'

Though such skilled mimics, they lack imagination. A sort of resigned wisdom, the peasant terror of adventure and distant travel, already keeps them all – the clock-maker's child, the grocer's little girl, and the offspring of the butcher and the laundress – chained to their parents' shops.

It is true that Jeanne roundly announced, 'I shall be a tart!'

'But that sort of thing', Minet-Chéri reflects contemptuously, 'is simply childish nonsense.'

Having no special wish when her turn came, she had thrown out with a certain contempt, 'I? Oh, I shall be a sailor!' And that was simply because she sometimes dreamed of being a boy, and wearing trousers and a blue beret. The sea, of which Minet-

Chéri knows nothing, the ship breasting a wave, the golden island, and the gleaming fruit, all that only surged up much later, to serve as a background to the blue blouse and the cap with a pom-pom.

'I shall be a sailor, and on my voyages . . .'

She sits down on the grass to rest and reflect. Travel? Adventure? For a child who, twice a year, at the periods of the great spring and winter provisioning, leaves the confines of her district, and drives in a victoria to her county town, such words have neither force nor value. They evoke only the printed page, the coloured picture. The Little One, now very tired, repeats the words 'When I go round the world . . .' automatically, just as she would say, 'When I go gathering chestnuts . . .'

In the house a lamp behind the sitting-room window suddenly glows red and the Little One shivers. All that had looked green up to the moment before, now turns blue around this motionless red flame. The child's hand, trailing in the grass, is suddenly aware of the evening damp. It is the hour of lamps. Leaves rustle together with a sound like the plash of running water and the door of the hayloft flaps against the wall as it does in a winter gale. The garden, grown suddenly hostile, menaces a now sobered little girl with the cold leaves of its laurels, the raised sabres of its yuccas, and the barbed caterpillars of its monkey-puzzle tree. A roar like the ocean comes from the direction of Moutiers where the wind, unchecked, runs in flurries over the tossing treetops. The Little One, sitting on the grass, keeps her eyes fixed on the lamp, veiled for a moment by a brief eclipse. A hand has passed in front of the flame, a hand wearing a shining thimble. At the mere sight of this hand the Little One starts to her feet, pale, gentle now, trembling slightly as a child must who for the first time ceases to be the happy little vampire that unconsciously drains the maternal heart; trembling slightly at the conscious realization that this hand and this flame, and the bent, anxious head beside the lamp, are the centre and the secret birthplace whence radiate in ripples ever less perceptible, in circles ever more and more remote from the essential light and its vibrations, the warm sitting-room with its flora of cut branches and its fauna of peaceful creatures; the echoing house, dry, warm, and crackling as a newly baked loaf; the garden, the village. . . . Beyond these all is danger, all is loneliness.

The 'sailor', with faltering steps, ventures upon *terra firma* and makes for the house, turning her back on an enormous yellow moon, just rising. Adventure? Travels? The enterprise that makes the emigrant? With her eyes glued to the shining thimble, to the hand that passes to and fro before the flame, Minet-Chéri savours the delicious contrition of being – like the clockmaker's child, like the little girls of the laundress and the baker – a child of her village, hostile alike to colonist and barbarian, one of those whose universe is bounded by the limits of a field, by the entrance of a shop, by the circle of light spreading beneath a lamp, and crossed at intervals by a well-loved hand drawing a thread and wearing a silver thimble.

Colette (1873–1954)

Ideas for discussion

- The Little One seems to hover between the security of her family and village and the excitement of the wider world. How does Colette convey this contest in the passage?

- The games played by the little girls seem to echo the society around them. How does Colette seem to view the village and its inhabitants?

- At the end of the passage, the garden becomes a strange and frightening place. Why do you think this is?

Suggestions for writing

Our memories of childhood often contain moments of sudden fear or happiness. Think back to your own childhood. Can you remember anything like Minet-Chéri's (The Little One's) experience in the garden?

Because memories like this are by their very nature intense and difficult to describe, you may find you need to fictionalise your account by adding in details that you do not actually remember.

● Ann Veronica Talks to her Father ●

When a young boy or girl reaches adolescence, he or she wants more independence. This often leads to family arguments, particularly in the case of girls who often have more difficulty persuading their parents that they are old enough to look after themselves. Nowadays, this battle is likely to take place at the age of fourteen or fifteen, but in the past girls were expected to be supervised by an adult chaperone until they were twenty-one. By the beginning of this century, young women were starting to rebel against this state of affairs.

When H. G. Wells wrote *Ann Veronica* in the early part of this century, he was taking part in the debate over what was called 'the New Woman'. Women wanted to play a major part in society which included the right to vote, to take advantage of higher education and the opportunity to pursue a career. Wells addresses these issues through the story of Ann Veronica, an intelligent and self-confident girl who, despite enormous opposition, eventually becomes a scientist. This extract describes the first skirmish in her battle for independence. She simply wants to go to a dance that involves an overnight stay in London. Her father has other ideas.

When Ann Veronica came into the study she found every evidence of a carefully foreseen grouping about the gas fire. Both arm-chairs had been moved a little so as to face each other on either side of the fender, and in the circular glow of the green-shaded lamp there lay, conspicuously waiting, a thick bundle of blue and white papers tied with pink tape. Her father held some printed document in his hand, and appeared not to observe her entry. 'Sit down,' he said, and perused – 'perused' is the word for it – for some moments. Then he put the paper by. 'And what is it all about, Veronica?' he asked with a deliberate note of irony, looking at her a little quizzically over his glasses.

Ann Veronica looked bright and a little elated, and she disregarded her father's invitation to be seated. She stood on the mat instead, and looked down on him. 'Look here, daddy', she said in a tone of great reasonableness, 'I *must* go to that dance, you know.'

Her father's irony deepened. 'Why?' he asked suavely.

Her answer was not quite ready. 'Well, because I don't see any reason why I shouldn't.'

'You see, I do.'

'Why shouldn't I go?'

'It isn't a suitable place; it isn't a suitable gathering.'

'But, daddy, what do you know of the place and the gathering?'

'And it's entirely out of order; it isn't right, it isn't correct; it's impossible for you to stay in an hotel in London – the idea is preposterous. I can't imagine what possessed you, Veronica.'

He put his head on one side, pulled down the corners of his mouth, and looked at her over his glasses.

'But why is it preposterous?' asked Ann Veronica, and fiddled with a pipe on the mantel.

'Surely!' he remarked, with an expression of worried appeal.

'You see, daddy, I don't think it *is* preposterous. That's really what I want to discuss. It comes to this – am I to be trusted to take care of myself, or am I not?'

'To judge from this proposal of yours, I should say not.'

'I think I am.'

'As long as you remain under my roof,' he began, and paused.

'You are going to treat me as though I wasn't. Well I don't think that's fair.'

'Your ideas of fairness,' he remarked, and discontinued that sentence. 'My dear girl,' he said in a tone of patient reasonableness, 'you are a mere child. You know nothing of life, nothing of its dangers, nothing of its possibilities. You think everything is harmless and simple, and so forth. It isn't. It isn't. That's where you go wrong. In some things, in many things, you must trust to your elders, to those who know more of life than you do. Your aunt and I have discussed all this matter. There it is. You can't go.'

The conversation hung for a moment. Ann Veronica tried to keep hold of a complicated situation and not lose her head. She had turned round sideways so as to look down into the fire.

'You see, father', she said, 'it isn't only this affair of the dance. I want to go to that because it's a new experience, because I think it will be interesting and give me a view of things. You say I know nothing. That's probably true. But how am I to know of things?'

'Some things I hope you may never know,' he said.

'I'm not so sure. I want to know – just as much as I can.'

'Tut!' he said fuming, and put out his hand to the papers in the pink tape.

'Well, I do. It's just that I want to say. I want to be a human being; I want to learn about things and know about things, and not to be protected as something too precious for life, cooped up in one narrow little corner.'

'Cooped up!' he cried. 'Did I stand in the way of your going to college? Have I ever prevented you going about at any reasonable hour? You've got a bicycle!'

'H'm!' said Ann Veronica, and then went on: 'I want to be taken seriously. A girl – at my age – is grown-up. I want to go on with my university work under proper conditions now that I've done the intermediate. It isn't as though I haven't done well. I've never muffed an exam yet. Roddy muffed two. . . '

Her father interrupted. 'Now look here, Veronica, let us be plain with each other. You are not going to that infidel Russell's classes. You are not going anywhere but to the Tredgold College. I've thought that out, and you must make up your mind to it. All sorts of considerations come in. While you live in my house you must follow my ideas. You are wrong even about that man's scientific position and his standard of work. There are men in the Lowndean who laugh at him – simply laugh at him. And I have seen work by his pupils myself that struck me as being – well, next door to shameful. There's stories, too, about his demonstrator, Capes. Something or other. The kind of man who isn't content with his science, and writes articles in the monthly reviews. Anyhow, there it is: *you are not going there.*'

The girl received this intimation in silence, but the face that looked down upon the gas fire took an expression of obstinacy that brought out a hitherto latent resemblance between parent and child. When she spoke her lips twitched.

'Then I suppose when I have graduated I am to come home?'

'It seems the natural course.'

'And do nothing?'

'There are plenty of things a girl can find to do at home.'

'Until some one takes pity on me and marries me?'

He raised his eyebrows in mild appeal. His foot tapped impatiently, and he took up the papers.

'Look here, father,' she said, with a change in her voice, 'suppose I won't stand it?'

He regarded her as though this was a new idea.

'Suppose, for example, I go to this dance?'

'You won't.'

'Well' – her breath failed her for a moment. 'How would you prevent it?' she asked.

'But I have forbidden it!' he said, raising his voice.

'Yes, I know. But suppose I go?'

'Now, Veronica! No, no. This won't do. Understand me! I forbid it. I do not want to hear from you even the threat of disobedience.' He spoke loudly. 'The thing is forbidden!'

'I am ready to give up anything that you show to be wrong.'

'You will give up anything I wish you to give up.'

They stared at one another through a pause, and both faces were flushed and obstinate.

She was trying by some wonderful, secret, and motionless gymnastics to restrain her tears. But when she spoke her lips quivered, and they came. 'I mean to go to that dance,' she blubbered. 'I mean to go to that dance. I meant to reason with you, but you won't reason. You're dogmatic.'

At the sight of her tears his expression changed to a mingling of triumph and concern. He stood up, apparently intending to put an arm about her, but she stepped back from him quickly. She produced a handkerchief, and with one sweep of this and a simultaneous gulp had abolished her fit of weeping. His voice now had lost it ironies.

'Now, Veronica,' he pleaded, 'Veronica, this is most unreasonable. All we do is for your good. Neither your aunt nor I have any other thought but what is best for you.'

'Only you won't let me live. Only you won't let me exist!'

Mr Stanley lost patience. He bullied frankly.

'What nonsense is this? What raving! My dear child, you *do* live, you *do* exist! You have this home. You have friends, acquaintances, social standing, brothers and sisters, every advantage! Instead of which, you want to go to some mixed classes or other and cut up rabbits and dance about at nights in wild costumes with casual art student friends and God knows who. That – that isn't living! You are beside yourself. You don't know what you ask, nor what you say. You have neither reason nor logic. I am sorry to seem to hurt you, but all I say is for your good. You *must* not, you *shall* not go. On this I am resolved. I put my foot down like – like adamant. And a time will come, Veronica, mark my words, a time will come when you will bless me for my firmness to-night. It goes to my heart to disappoint you, but this thing must not be.'

He sidled towards her, but she recoiled from him, leaving him in possession of the hearthrug.

'Well,' she said, 'good night, father.'

'What!' he asked; 'not a kiss?'

She affected not to hear.

The door closed softly upon her. For a long time he remained standing before the fire, staring at the situation. Then he sat down and filled his pipe slowly and thoughtfully. . .

'I don't see what else I could have said,' he remarked.

H. G. Wells (1866–1946)

Ideas for discussion

- Why do you think this chapter is called 'Ann Veronica Talks to her Father' and not 'Mr Stanley Talks to his Daughter'?

- At the end of the conversation, Mr Stanley says that Ann Veronica has 'neither reason nor logic'. Who seems to you the more unreasonable? Why is this?

- What are Ann Veronica's tactics during the argument? Do you think she tackles it in the right way?

- At the beginning of the passage it is obvious that Mr Stanley has 'stage-managed' the conversation. How do you think he wanted it to go?

- Why do you think Ann Veronica feels it is so important for her not to cry?

- Ann Veronica does go to the dance. In fact, she climbs out of her bedroom window and goes without telling her father. How do you think he would react to this?

Suggestions for writing

1 Write a modern version of an argument like this between a daughter and her father or mother.

2 Do you think that parents allow sons more freedom than daughters? If so, do you feel this is right? Write an essay in which you express your views on the subject.

• A Visit From Lupin •

Ann Veronica deals with family difficulties from the young person's point of view but *The Diary of a Nobody*, published in 1892, sees things through the eyes of Mr Pooter, an absurd character who is totally unable to understand the rest of his family, least of all his son, William.

This book, written by two brothers, George and Walter Weedon Grossmith, was the first of a popular genre – the comic diary – modern examples of which are *The Secret Diary of Adrian Mole* and *Diary of a Teenage Health Freak*.

In this extract, Mr and Mrs Pooter receive a visit from their son, Willie. At least, that is what he *used* to call himself.

AUGUST 5, SUNDAY. We have not seen Willie since last Christmas, and are pleased to notice what a fine young man he has grown. One would scarcely believe he was Carrie's son. He looks more like a younger brother. I rather disapprove of his wearing a check suit on a Sunday, and I think he ought to have gone to church this morning; but he said he was tired after yesterday's journey, so I refrained from any remark on the subject. We had a bottle of port for dinner, and drank dear Willie's health.

He said: 'Oh, by-the-by, did I tell you I've cut my first name, "William", and taken the second name "Lupin"? In fact, I'm only known at Oldham as "Lupin Pooter". If you were to "Willie" me there, they wouldn't know what you meant.'

Of course, Lupin being a purely family name, Carrie was delighted, and began by giving a long history of the Lupins. I ventured to say that I thought William a nice simple name, and reminded him he was christened after his uncle William, who was much respected in the City. Willie, in a manner which I did not much care for, said sneeringly: 'Oh, I know all about that – Good old Bill!' and helped himself to a third glass of port.

Carrie objected strongly to my saying 'Good old', but she made no remark when Willie used the double adjective. I said nothing, but looked at her, which meant more. I said: 'My dear Willie, I hope you are happy with your colleagues at the Bank.' He replied: 'Lupin, if you please; and with respect to the Bank, there's not a clerk who is a gentleman, and the "boss" is a cad.' I felt so shocked, I could say nothing, and my instinct told me there was something wrong.

Lupin.

AUGUST 6, BANK HOLIDAY. As there was no sign of Lupin moving at nine o'clock, I knocked at his door, and said we usually breakfasted at half-past eight, and asked how long would he be? Lupin replied that he had had a lively time of it, first with the trains shaking the house all night, and then with the sun streaming in through the window in his eyes, and giving him a cracking headache. Carrie came up and asked if he would like some breakfast sent up, and he said he could do with a cup of tea, and didn't want anything to eat.

Lupin not having come down, I went up again at half-past one, and said we dined at two; he said he 'would be there'. He never came down till a quarter to three. I said: 'We have not seen much of you, and you will have to return by the 5.30 train; therefore you will have to leave in an hour, unless you go by the midnight mail.' He said: 'Look here, Guv'nor, it's no use beating about the bush. I've tendered my resignation at the Bank.'

For a moment I could not speak. When my speech came again, I said: 'How dare you, sir? How dare you take such a serious step without consulting me? Don't answer me, sir! – you will sit down immediately, and write a note at my dictation, withdrawing your resignation and amply apologizing for your thoughtlessness.'

Imagine my dismay when he replied with a loud guffaw: 'It's no use. If you want the good old truth, I've got the chuck!'

AUGUST 11. Although it is a serious matter having our boy Lupin on our hands, still it is satisfactory to know he was asked to resign from the Bank simply because 'he took no interest in his work, and always arrived an hour (sometimes two hours) late.' We can all start off on Monday to Broadstairs with a light heart. This will take my mind off the worry of the last few days, which have been wasted over a useless correspondence with the manager of the Bank at Oldham.

AUGUST 13. Hurrah! at Broadstairs. Very nice apartments near the station. On the cliffs they would have been double the price. The landlady had a nice five o'clock dinner and tea ready, which we all enjoyed, though Lupin seemed fastidious because there happened to be a fly in the butter. It was very wet in the evening, for which I was thankful, as it was a good excuse for going to bed early. Lupin said he would sit up and read a bit.

AUGUST 14. I was a little annoyed to find Lupin, instead of reading last night, had gone to a common sort of entertainment, given at the Assembly Rooms. I expressed my opinion that such performances were unworthy of respectable patronage; but he replied: 'Oh, it was only "for one night only". I had a fit of the blues come on, and thought I would go to see Polly Presswell, England's Particular Spark.' I told him I was proud to say I had never heard of her. Carrie said: 'Do let the boy alone. He's quite old enough to take care of himself, and won't forget he's a gentleman. Remember, you were young once yourself.' Rained all day hard, but Lupin would go out.

AUGUST 15. Cleared up a bit, so we all took the train to Margate, and the first person we met on the jetty was Gowing. I said: 'Hulloh! I though you had gone to Barmouth with your Birmingham friends.' He said: 'Yes, but young Peter Lawrence was so ill, they postponed their visit, so I came down here. You know the Cummings are here too?' Carrie said. 'Oh, that will be delightful! We must have some evenings together and have games.'

I introduced Lupin, saying: 'You will be pleased to find we have our dear boy at home!' Gowing said: 'How's that? You don't mean to say he's left the Bank?'

I changed the subject quickly, and thereby avoided any of those awkward questions which Gowing always has a knack of asking.

AUGUST 16. Lupin positively refused to walk down the Parade with me because I was wearing my new straw helmet with my frock-coat. I don't know what the boy is coming to.

AUGUST 18. Gowing and Cummings walked over to arrange an evening at Margate. It being wet, Gowing asked Cummings to accompany him to the hotel and have a game of billiards, knowing I never play, and in fact disapprove of the game. Cummings said he must hasten back to Margate; whereupon Lupin, to my horror, said 'I'll give you a game, Gowing – a hundred up. A walk round the cloth will give me an appetite for dinner.' I said: 'Perhaps *Mister* Gowing does not care to play with boys.' Gowing surprised me by saying: 'Oh yes, I do, if they play well,' and they walked off together.

AUGUST 19, SUNDAY. I was about to read Lupin a sermon on smoking (which he indulges in violently) and billiards, but he put on his hat and walked out. Carrie then read *me* a long sermon on the palpable inadvisability of treating Lupin as if he were a mere child. I felt she was somewhat right, so in the evening I offered him a cigar. He seemed pleased, but, after a few whiffs, said: 'This is a good old tup'ny – try one of mine,' and he handed me a cigar as long as it was strong, which is saying a good deal.

George and Walter Weedon Grossmith (1847–1912 and 1854–1919)

Ideas for discussion

- Mr Pooter and his son seem to live in different worlds and to speak different languages. Why is this?
- What do you think Mrs Pooter's views are?
- Do you find this extract funny? If so, work out what it is that makes you laugh.

Suggestions for writing

Write your own version of a comic diary. Here are some ideas to help you:

- The Diary of a Teacher – a teacher who cannot understand why his or her pupils will not do as they are told.
- The Diary of Mr or Ms Supercool – a young boy or girl who thinks him/herself to be the trendiest thing on two legs and cannot understand why the others laugh.
- The Diary of a Young Nobody – an updated version of the original. A few days in the life of an ordinary school student (someone who sits at the back of the class and seems to be invisible as far as teachers are concerned).

unit 2

Love

Love has inspired more people to write than almost any other subject.

This unit charts the course of love from the joy of first meetings to the sadness of separation.

Spring's about

The beginning of a relationship is always a gamble. The thoughts that go through our heads are: What if I pick the wrong person? What if I am rejected? Am I being pressured into a relationship that I do not want? These three poems explore this difficult time.

Winter: My Secret

I tell my secret? No indeed, not I:
Perhaps some day, who knows?
But not to-day; it froze, and blows, and snows
And you're too curious: fie!
You want to hear it? well:
Only, my secret's mine, and I won't tell.

Or, after all, perhaps there's none:
Suppose there is no secret after all,
But only just my fun.
To-day's a nipping day, a biting day;
In which one wants a shawl,
A veil, a cloak, and other wraps:
I cannot ope to every one who taps,
And let the draughts come whistling through my hall;
Come bounding and surrounding me,
Come buffeting, astounding me,
Nipping and clipping through my wraps and all.
I wear my mask for warmth: who ever shows
His nose to Russian snows
To be pecked at by every wind that blows?
You would not peck? I thank you for good will.
Believe, but leave that truth untested still.

Spring's an expansive time: yet I don't trust
March with its peck of dust,
Nor April with its rainbow-crowned brief showers,
Nor even May, whose flowers
One frost may wither through the sunless hours.

Perhaps some languid summer day,
When drowsy birds sing less and less,
And golden fruit is ripening to excess,
If there's not much sun nor too much cloud,
And the warm wind is neither still nor loud,
Perhaps my secret I may say,
Or you may guess.

Christina Rossetti (1830–1894)

Here are some ideas to help you think about 'Winter: My Secret' which is quite a complex poem:

Think of the poem as one side of a dialogue between the poet and a friend (perhaps a man). Try to supply the friend's words.

Think about what we mean by openness between people. How is this idea represented in the poem?

What kind of tone of voice does Rossetti employ in the poem?

Spring's about with love again

Spring's about with love again,
With blossom and with birds' refrain
   The top of pleasure bringing.
Daisies whitening all the dales,
The lovely notes of nightingales –
   Every bird is singing.
The song-thrush endlessly trills on,
For winter's misery is gone
   When the woodruff's springing.
A host of birds profusely sing
The joy and blessing of the spring,
   And set the woodlands ringing.

The rose puts on her reddening hue,
The leaves with ardour sprout anew,
   In the bright woods glowing.
The moon sends down her radiant light,
While lilies, lovely to the sight,
   Fennel and thyme are blowing.
Wild and wanton drakes abound;
Their mating calls to lovers sound
   Like stream serenely flowing.
The passionate man and others sigh,
And of that company am I,
   Distraught with love and wooing.

The moonbeams shed their lovely light,
And when the glorious sun shines bright,
  The sounds of bird-song swell.
The moistening dew on uplands falls,
Creatures utter secret calls,
  Their loving tales to tell.
Worms beneath the ground make love;
Women flaunt their pride above –
  The spring becomes them well.
If none of them can burn for me,
Then, lost to fortune, I shall flee
  And in the wild wood dwell.

*Anon. (Written between 1264 and
1314. It has been translated from
the Middle English.)*

Love's Philosophy

The fountains mingle with the river
And the rivers with the ocean,
The winds of heaven mix for ever
With a sweet emotion;
Nothing in the world is single,
All things by a law divine
In one another's being mingle –
Why not I with thine?

See the mountains kiss high heaven
And the waves clasp one another;
No sister-flower would be forgiven
It it disdain'd its brother:
And the sunlight clasps the earth.
And the moonbeams kiss the sea –
What are all these kissings worth,
If thou kiss not me?

Percy Bysshe Shelley (1792–1822)

Ideas for discussion

- Each poet in this section compares his or her feelings with the natural world. Examine each poem in turn and discuss how the poet uses nature.

- What kind of experience do you think has led to the writing of each poem? Find evidence in the poems to back up your ideas.

- What kind of relationship does each poet desire?

- Which poet seems most in control of his or her feelings?

- Which poem seems to you:
  the most personal?
  the most convincing?
  the most honest?

Suggestions for writing

1 Use the ideas that came up in your discussions of the poems to write an essay in which you compare the ways in which the three poets express their feelings.
2 The writer of 'Spring's about. . .' seems to feel that everyone is falling in love except him. He looks around and sees the world divided into couples. He seems terribly afraid that he will be left out.

    Write a modern interpretation of this idea in the form of a story in which a young boy or girl feels left out when it seems that everyone else is pairing off. Write from her or his point of view and explore the way she or he might feel.

The moment

These four poems explore that exciting moment when love is reciprocated. The fear or rejection has disappeared and the lovers can feel secure in each other's arms.

Love and Sleep

Lying asleep between the strokes of night
   I saw my love lean over my sad bed,
   Pale as the duskiest lily's leaf or head,
Smooth-skinned and dark, with bare throat made to bite,
Too wan for blushing and too warm for white,
    But perfect-coloured without white or red.
    And her lips opened amorously, and said –
I wist not what, saving one word – Delight.

And all her face was honey to my mouth,
    And all her body pasture to mine eyes;
      The long lithe arms and hotter hands than fire,
The quivering flanks, hair smelling of the south,
    The bright light feet, the splendid supple thighs
      And glittering eyelids of my soul's desire.

Algernon Charles Swinburne (1837–1909)

Elegia V

Corinnae concubitus

In summer's heat, and mid-time of the day,
To rest my limbs upon a bed I lay;
One window shut, the other open stood,
Which gave such light as twinkles in a wood,
Like twilight glimpse at setting of the sun,
Or night being past, and yet not day begun.
Such light to shamefast maidens must be shown,
Where they may sport and seem to be unknown.
Then came Corinna in a long loose gown,
Her white neck hid with tresses hanging down,
Resembling fair Semiramis going to bed,
Or Lais of a thousand wooers sped.
I snatched her gown; being thin, the harm was small,
Yet strived she to be covered therewithal,
And striving thus as one that would be cast,
Betrayed herself, and yielded at the last.
Stark naked as she stood before mine eye,
Not one wen in her body could I spy.
What arms and shoulders did I touch and see,
How apt her breasts were to be pressed by me!
How smooth a belly under her waist saw I,
How large a leg, and what a lusty thigh!
To leave the rest, all liked me passing well;
I clinged her naked body, down she fell.
Judge you the rest: being tired she bade me kiss;
Jove send me more such afternoons as this.

Ovid (43 B.C.–A.D. 17), translated by
Christopher Marlowe (1564–1593)

Song: The Willing Mistriss

Amyntas led me to a grove
   Where all the trees did shade us;
The sun itself, though it had strove,
   It could not have betrayed us:
The place secured from human eyes,
   No other fear allows,
But when the winds that gently rise,
   Does kiss the yielding boughs.

Down there we sat upon the moss,
   And did begin to play
A thousand amorous tricks, to pass
   The heat of all the day.
A many kisses he did give;
   And I returned the same
Which made me willing to receive
   That which I dare not name.

His charming eyes no aid required
   To tell their soft'ning tale;
On her that was already fired
   'Twas easy to prevail.
He did but kiss and clasp me round,
   Whilst those his thoughts expressed:
   And laid me gently on the ground;
   Ah who can guess the rest?

Aphra Behn (1640–1689)

part of *'Juan and Haidee'* from *Don Juan* (verses 184 – 188)

And thus they wandered forth, and hand in hand,
  Over the shining pebbles and the shells,
Glided along the smooth and hardened sand,
  And in the worn and wild receptacles
Worked by the storms, yet worked as it were planned,
  In hollow halls with sparry roofs and cells,
They turned to rest, and each clasped by an arm,
Yielded to the deep twilight's purple charm.

They looked up to the sky, whose floating glow
  Spread like a rosy ocean, vast and bright.
They gazed upon the glittering sea below,
  Whence the broad moon rose circling into sight.
They heard the wave's splash and the wind so low,
  And saw each other's dark eyes darting light
Into each other, and beholding this,
Their lips drew near and clung into a kiss,

A long, long kiss, a kiss of youth and love
  And beauty, all concentrating like rays
Into one focus, kindled from above;
  Such kisses as belong to early days,
Where heart and soul and sense in concert move,
  And the blood's lava, and the pulse a blaze,
Each kiss a heart-quake, for a kiss's strength,
I think, it must be reckoned by its length.

By length I mean duration; theirs endured
  Heaven knows how long; no doubt they never reckoned,
And if they had, they could not have secured
  The sum of their sensations to a second.
They had not spoken, but they felt allured,
  As if their souls and lips each other beckoned,
Which, being joined, like swarming bees they clung,
Their hearts the flowers from whence the honey sprung.

They were alone, but not alone as they
  Who shut in chambers think it loneliness.
The silent ocean and the starlight bay,
  The twilight glow, which momently grew less,
The voiceless sands and dropping caves, that lay
  Around them, made them to each other press,
As if there were no life beneath the sky
Save theirs, and that their life could never die.

Lord Byron (1788–1824)

Ideas for discussion

■ These poems deal frankly with sex. Three of them are by men and only one by a women (Aphra Behn). It is very rare to find such an explicit poem written by a woman before this century. Why do you think this is?

■ The first three poems deal with sexual encounters in a similar way. Does Aphra Behn's poem 'Song: The Willing Mistriss' differ from the Swinburne or Ovid? Is it obvious that it is by a woman?

■ Byron's poem is different from the other three in that it is narrated in the third person. It describes the lovers from the outside, so to speak. We are not told their thoughts. What kind of picture does Byron paint of their encounter?

Suggestions for writing

1 You may have been surprised to find such frank depictions of sex written before this century — Ovid was born in 43 BC and the translation is sixteenth century; Aphra Behn wrote in the eighteenth century and Swinburne was a Victorian. We tend to think of our own century as being the most sexually liberated, but this is not strictly true. Over the centuries people's attitudes to sexually explicit literature have changed many times.

   Do you think that writing of this kind is in poor taste? If not, how would you defend it? Is it little more than literary pornography or a mature expression of genuine emotion?

   Write an essay in which you express your views on whether these poems are acceptable or not.

2 Byron's description of lovers in their own world is one of the first versions of an image which has been copied many times since. How often have you come across lovers on a beach at twilight in books or on the screen? Is it possible to write a description of a romantic scene without it becoming clichéd or sounding like a shampoo advert?

   Try writing a scene like this yourself. Remember that the scenery is almost as important as the lovers.

The end

The following five poems deal with the ends of love affairs. In some cases the lovers have simply fallen out of love; in others they have been separated tragically by death.

We'll go no more a-roving

So, we'll go no more a-roving
  So late into the night,
Though the heart be still as loving,
  And the moon be still as bright.

For the sword outwears it sheath,
  And the soul wears out the breast,
And the heart must pause to breathe,
  And love itself have rest.

Though the night was made for loving,
  And the day returns too soon,
Yet we'll go no more a-roving
  By the light of the moon.

Lord Byron (1788–1824)

Since there's no help

Since there's no help, come let us kiss and part.
  Nay, I have done; you get no more of me,
And I am glad, yea, glad with all my heart,
  That thus so cleanly I myself can free;
Shake hands for ever, cancel all our vows,
  And when we meet at any time again,
Be it not seen in either of our brows
  That we one jot of former love retain.
Now at the last gasp of Love's latest breath,
  When, his pulse failing, Passion speechless lies,
When Faith is kneeling by his bed of death,
  And Innocence is closing up his eyes,
    Now if thou wouldst, when all have given him over,
    From death to life though might'st him yet recover.

Michael Drayton (1563–1631)

I must go walke the woed

I must go walke the woed so wild
And wander here and there
In dred and dedly fere,
For where I trusted I am begild,
And all for one.

Thus am I banished from my blis
By craft and false pretens,
Fautless, without offens,
As of return no certen is,
And all for fer of one.

My bed shall be under the grenwod tree,
A tuft of brakes under my hed,
As one from joye were fled.
Thus from my lif day by day I flee,
And all for one.

The ronning stremes shall be my drinke,
Acorns shall be my fode:
Nothing may do me good,
But when of your bewty I do think,
And all for love of one.

Anon (written about 1500)

certen   *certainty*
lif   *beloved, source of my life*

The Lost Love

She dwelt among the untrodden ways
  Beside the springs of Dove;
A maid whom there were none to praise,
  And very few to love.

A violet by a mossy stone
  Half-hidden from the eye!
– Fair as a star, when only one
  Is shining in the sky.

She lived unknown, and few could know
When Lucy ceased to be;
But she is in her grave, and O!
  The difference to me!

William Wordsworth (1770–1850)

Arthur O'Leary, an Irish colonel in the Austrian army was outlawed and killed in Country Cork, Ireland, in 1773 for refusing to sell his mare to a Protestant (Catholics were not permitted by law to possess valuable horses). This is the first part of a lament written by his wife. It has been translated from the original Irish.

The Lament for Art O'Leary

My love and my delight,
The day I saw you first
Beside the market-house
I had eyes for nothing else
And love for none but you.

I left my father's house
And ran away with you,
And that was no bad choice;
You gave me everything.

There were parlours whitened for me,
Bedrooms painted for me,
Ovens reddened for me,
Loaves baked for me,
Joints spitted for me,
Beds made for me
To take my ease on flock
Until the milking time
And later if I pleased.

My mind remembers
That bright spring day,
How your hat with its band
Of gold became you,
Your silver-hilted sword,
Your manly right hand,
Your horse on her mettle
And foes around you
Cowed by your air;
For when you rode by
On your white-nosed mare
The English lowered their head before you
Not out of love for you
But hate and fear,
For, sweetheart of my soul,
The English killed you.

My love and my calf
Of the race of the Earls of Antrim
And the Barrys of Eemokilly,
How well a sword became you,
A hat with a band,
A slender foreign shoe
And a suit of yarn
Woven over the water!

My love and my darling
When I go home
The little lad, Conor,
And Fiach the baby
Will surely ask me
Where I left their father,
I'll say with anguish
'Twas in Kilnamartyr;
They will call the father
Who will never answer.

My love and my mate
That I never thought dead
Till your horse came to me
With bridle trailing,
All blood from forehead
To polished saddle
Where you should be,
Either sitting or standing;
I gave one leap to the threshold,
A second to the gate,
A third upon its back.

I clapped my hands,
And off at a gallop;
I never lingered
Till I found you lying
By a little furze-bush
Without pope or bishop
Or priest or cleric
One prayer to whisper
But an old, old woman,
And her cloak about you,
And your blood in torrents –
Art O'Leary –
I did not wipe it off,
I drank it from my palms.

My love and my delight
Stand up now beside me,
And let me lead you home
Until I make a feast,
And I will roast the meat
And send for company
And call the harpers in,
And I shall make your bed
Of soft and snowy sheets
And blankets dark and rough
To warm the beloved limbs
An autumn blast has chilled.

Eileen O'Leary (dates unknown)

Ideas for discussion

- Look closely at 'We'll go no more a-roving' and 'Since there's no help. . .'. How do the poets feel about the ending of their love affairs?

- In 'I must go walke the woed', the poet expresses his feelings of rejection when he discovers that his lover has been unfaithful. Turn to page 40 and compare it with 'Spring's about with love again'. How do the poets use nature to echo their mood?

- 'The Lost Love' and 'The Lament for Art O'Leary' both express the pain of loss. How do the poets convey their grief?

Suggestions for writing

1 Byron's poem is an attempt to end a relationship that seems to have gone stale. There is no passion in it, only a sense of weary resignation. Write a story in which someone attempts to end a relationship which no longer sparkles as it did. You could read 'The End of Something', a short story by Ernest Hemingway, to see how another writer tackled a similar subject.

2 Drayton's sonnet seems to describe how glad he is to end a love affair, but he gives himself away at the end. He is really pleading for the relationship to continue, but is too proud to say so. He has to hide his true feelings behind a false expression of not caring.

   Write a story or play script in which this complex mixture of feelings is portrayed in a modern setting. A young man or woman really wants a relationship to continue, but is too proud to say so. What does the other partner want?

3 'The Lament for Art O'Leary' is a sad story of love that ends tragically. Eileen O'Leary paints a vivid picture of the various stages of her relationship with Art. Write your own prose version of an episode from the story. For example, you could choose to describe Eileen's first sight of Art or her running away with him.

The eyes of love

We often talk about people falling in love 'at first sight'. This section contains three extracts from novels in which love is focused through the eyes of the characters, and looking and observing are the first steps to love.

Does the watcher have power over the person he or she is watching, or is it the other way round? Before you read the extracts, discuss the following statements:

- Watching someone gives you power over them.
- It makes a difference if you know you are being watched.
- Watching someone is an attempt to possess them.
- Watching someone without their knowledge is immoral.
- Men watch women differently from the way women watch men.

Now, as you read each extract, think about which of the characters is the more powerful. Does any character come across as a victim?

• First Love •

First Love by Ivan Turgenev was written in the 1850s and concerns the growing awareness of young Vladimir who, at the age of sixteen, falls in love with his next-door neighbour.

In this extract, he tells of his first sight of Zinaida.

I was in the habit of wandering about our garden every evening with a gun looking for crows. I had an inveterate loathing for these wary, cunning and predatory birds. On the day in question I strolled as usual into the garden and, having scoured every walk in vain (the crows knew me and only cawed harshly now and then from afar), I happened to come near the low fence which divided 'our' property from the narrow strip of garden which ran to the right beyond the lodge and belonged to it. I was walking with my head bowed when suddenly I heard the sound of voices. I looked across the fence – and stood transfixed. A strange sight met my gaze.

A few paces from me – on a lawn flanked by green raspberry canes – stood a tall, slender girl in a striped pink dress with a white kerchief on her head. Four young men clustered round her, and she was tapping them one by one on the forehead with those small grey flowers – I do not know their name, but they are well known to children: these flowers form little bags and burst loudly if you strike them against anything hard. The young men offered their foreheads so eagerly, and there was in the girl's movements (I saw her in profile) something so enchanting, imperious and caressing, so mocking and charming, that I nearly cried out with wonder and delight, and should, I suppose, at that moment, have given everything in the world to have those lovely fingers tap my forehead too. My rifle slipped to the grass; I forgot everything; my eyes devoured the graceful figure, the lovely neck, the beautiful arms, the slightly dishevelled fair hair under the white kerchief – and the half-closed, perceptive eye, the lashes, the soft cheek beneath them. . .

'Young man! Hey, young man!' suddenly cried a voice near me. 'Is it proper to stare at unknown young ladies like that?'

I started violently, and almost fainted: near me, on the other side of the fence, stood a man with close-cropped dark hair, looking at me ironically. At the same moment the girl too turned towards me. . .I saw large grey eyes in a bright, lively face, and suddenly this face began to quiver and laugh. There was a gleam of white teeth, a droll lift of the eyebrows . . . I blushed terribly, snatched up my gun, and pursued by resonant but not unkind laughter, fled to my room, threw myself on the bed and covered my face with my hands. My heart leaped within me. I felt very ashamed and unusually gay. I was extraordinarily excited.

After a rest I combed my hair, brushed myself, and came down to tea. The image of the young girl floated before me. My heart was leaping no longer but felt somehow deliciously constricted. 'What is the matter with you,' my father asked suddenly. 'Shot a crow?' I nearly told him everything, but checked the impulse and only smiled to myself. As I was going to bed, without quite knowing why, I spun round two or three times on one foot; then I put pomade on my hair, lay down, and slept like a top all night. Before morning I woke up for an instant, lifted my head, looked round me in ecstacy and fell asleep again.

Ivan Turgenev (1818–1883)

Ideas for discussion

- In this extract, Turgenev is attempting to describe the feelings of a sixteen year old in love. Do you think he succeeds? Discuss how effectively you think the passage conveys Vladimir's emotions.

- What impression does the reader get of Zinaida's character? How successful do you think Vladimir will be in wooing her?

Suggestions for writing

Write your own 'First Love' story in which you describe the thoughts and feelings of a sixteen year old in love for the first time.

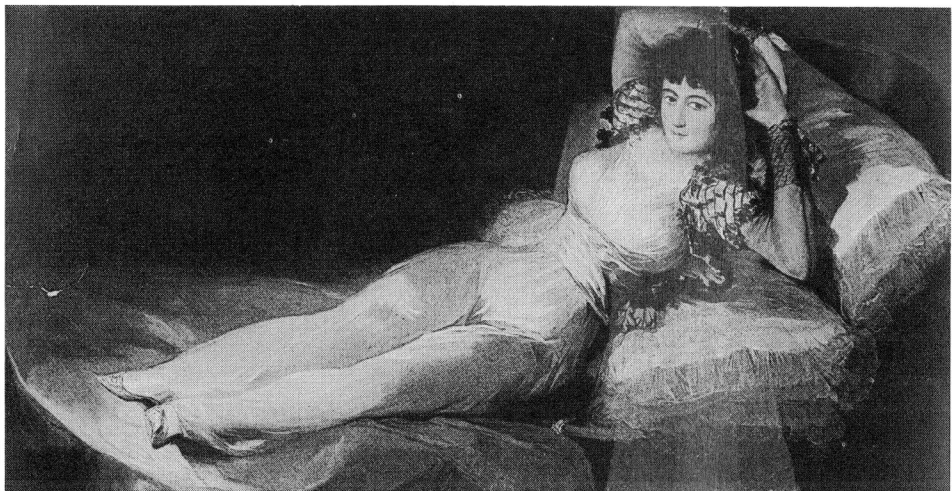

• Milking •

The following extract from Thomas Hardy's *Tess of the D'Urbervilles* takes place at the height of summer in Talbothays Dairy. Tess is employed as a milkmaid and on this particular afternoon she is being observed by Angel Clare, who, after rebelling against his parents' plans to send him to Cambridge, has come to the farm to study dairy farming.

On one of these afternoons four or five unmilked cows chanced to stand apart from the general herd, behind the corner of a hedge, among them being Dumpling and Old Pretty, who loved Tess's hands above those of any other maid. When she rose from her stool under a finished cow Angel Clare, who had been observing her for some time, asked her if she would take the aforesaid creatures next. She silently assented, and with her stool at arm's length, and the pail against her knee, went round to where they stood. Soon the sound of Old Pretty's milk fizzing into the pail came through the hedge, and then Angel felt inclined to go round the corner also, to finish off a hard-yielding milcher who had strayed there, he being now as capable of this as the dairyman himself.

All the men, and some of the women, when milking, dug their foreheads into the cows and gazed into the pail. But a few – mainly the younger ones – rested their heads sideways. This was Tess Durbeyfield's habit, her temple pressing the milcher's flank, her eyes fixed on the far end of the meadow with the quiet of one lost in meditation. She was milking Old Pretty thus, and the sun chancing to be on the milking-side it shone flat upon her pink-gowned form and her white curtain-bonnet, and upon her profile, rendering it keen as a cameo cut from the dun background of the cow.

She did not know that Clare had followed her round, and that he sat under his cow watching her. The stillness of her head and features was remarkable: she might have been in a trance, her eyes open, yet unseeing. Nothing in the picture moved but Old Pretty's tail and Tess's pink hands, the latter so gently as to be a rhythmic pulsation only, as if they were obeying a reflex stimulus, like a beating heart.

How very lovable her face was to him. Yet there was nothing ethereal about it; all was real vitality, real warmth, real incarnation. And it was in her mouth that this culminated. Eyes almost as deep and speaking he had seen before, and cheeks perhaps as fair; brows as arched, a chin and throat almost as shapely; her mouth he had seen nothing to equal on the face of the earth. To a young man with the least fire in him that little upward lift in the middle of her red top lip was distracting, infatuating, maddening. He had never before seen a woman's lips and teeth which forced upon his mind with such persistent iteration the old Elizabethan simile of roses filled with snow. Perfect, he, as a lover, might have called them off-hand. But no – they were not perfect. And it was the touch of the imperfect upon the would-be perfect that gave the sweetness, because it was that which gave the humanity.

Clare had studied the curves of those lips so many times that he could reproduce them mentally with ease: and now, as they again confronted him, clothed with colour and life, they sent an *aura* over his flesh, a breeze through his nerves, which wellnigh produced a qualm; and actually produced, by some mysterious physiological process, a prosaic sneeze.

She then became conscious that he was observing her; but she would not show it by any change of position, though the curious dream-like fixity disappeared, and a close eye might easily have discerned that the rosiness of her face deepened, and then faded till only a tinge of it was left.

The influence that had passed into Clare like an excitation from the sky did not die down. Resolutions, reticences, prudences, fears, fell back like a defeated battalion. He jumped up from his seat, and, leaving his pail to be kicked over if the milcher had such a mind, went quickly towards the desire of his eyes, and, kneeling down beside her, clasped her in his arms.

Tess was taken completely by surprise, and she yielded to his embrace with unreflecting inevitableness. Having seen that it was really her lover who had advanced, and no one else, her lips parted, and she sank upon him in her momentary joy, with something very like an ecstatic cry.

He had been on the point of kissing that too tempting mouth, but he checked himself, for tender conscience' sake.

'Forgive me, Tess dear!' he whispered. 'I ought to have asked. I – did not know what I was doing. I do not mean it as a liberty. I am devoted to you, Tessy, dearest, in all sincerity!'

Old Pretty by this time had looked round, puzzled; and seeing two people crouching under her where, by immemorial custom, there should have been only one, lifted her hind leg crossly.

'She is angry – she doesn't know what we mean – she'll kick over the milk!' exclaimed Tess, gently striving to free herself, her eyes concerned with the quadruped's actions, her heart more deeply concerned with herself and Clare.

She slipped up from her seat, and they stood together, his arm still encircling her. Tess's eyes, fixed on distance, began to fill.

'Why do you cry, my darling?' he said.

'O – I don't know!' she murmured.

As she saw and felt more clearly the position she was in she became agitated and tried to withdraw.

'Well, I have betrayed my feeling, Tess, at last,' said he, with a curious sigh of desperation, signifying unconsciously that his heart had outrun his judgment. 'That I – love you dearly and truly I need not say. But I – it shall go no further now – it distresses you – I am as surprised as you are. You will not think I have presumed upon your defencelessness – been too quick and unreflecting, will you?'

'N' – I can't tell.'

He had allowed her to free herself; and in a minute or two the milking of each was resumed. Nobody had beheld the gravitation of the two into one; and when the dairyman came round by that screened nook a few minutes later there was not a sign to reveal that the markedly sundered pair were more to each other than mere acquaintance. Yet in the interval since Crick's last view of them something had occurred which changed the pivot of the universe for their two natures; something which, had he known its quality, the dairyman would have despised, as a practical man; yet which was based upon a more stubborn and resistless tendency than a whole heap of so-called practicalities. A veil had been whisked aside; the tract of each one's outlook was to have a new horizon thenceforward – for a short time or for a long.

Thomas Hardy (1840–1928)

Ideas for discussion

- In this extract, Angel says much more than Tess. Look at what the two characters say and the way in which they say it. What does this tell us about their personalities?

- Discuss these statements about the extract. Which of them do you agree with? Back up your decisions with evidence from the text.

  - Angel acts impetuously.

  - Angel does not know Tess.

  - Tess is frightened of Angel.

  - Tess and Angel are unequal.

  - Tess is more of a realist than Angel.

  - Angel loves Tess.

  - Angel only thinks he loves Tess.

  - We do not know what Tess is thinking.

  - Tess is happy that Angel has declared his love.

Suggestions for writing

1 We know little of what is going through Tess's mind during this encounter. All we know is that she seems to be happy at first and then, later, she is in tears. Re-read the extract carefully and write a version of what might be going through Tess's mind at the end of the extract after she has gone back to her milking.

2 Imagine that Angel goes back to his family and tells them that he wishes to marry a milkmaid. His father is a vicar; how will he and his wife react to the news? How will Angel try to persuade them to accept the match? Write a version of this scene.

3 How would Angel describe Tess to a student friend? Write a scene in which Angel tells his best friend about his love. Think about the kind of picture he would paint of Tess. Would he tell the whole truth when he describes the encounter in the dairy?

• Raising Venus •

Precious Bane by Mary Webb is set in a remote part of rural England during the nineteenth century. It tells the story of Prudence Sarn who is born with a hare-lip; at that time, there were many superstitions surrounding this condition, and Mary is ostracised from her community because of it. She is constantly told that she will never have a lover. However, she falls in love with a local man, Kester Woodseaves.

In this extract, she takes part in a piece of fake magic conjured up by the local wizard, Beguildy. He claims that he can summon up the spirit of Venus, the goddess of love, and he invites the local gentry to watch. However, his daughter, Jancis, who was to have played the part of Venus, is too shy to do so, and she manages to persuade Prudence to take her place.

Serious-minded folk will need to pass over this raising of Venus, but I will shorten it as well as I can. It seemed a dreadful thing to me, as I set forth when the evening came, that I should be going to show myself stark naked. For though I knew that Miss Dorabella and other grand ladies did take off the tops of their gowns, evenings, and come forth half bare, and think it no shame, yet women of our sort have more chariness of themselves.

As I went in by the garden way, through the door on the low level, not to be seen, I was all of a tremble, and it was only the pitifulness of poor Jancis that made me go through with it. We could hear Beguildy moving about up above, opening the trap-door and putting all ready. I thought what a silly old man he was, to think anybody believed in his May-games. Then we heard young Mister Camperdine's horse, and there was a shuffling of feet above, and Beguildy pulled on the rope to show all was ready.

Oftentimes it is easier to die for love's sake than to be made a fool for love's sake. So I thought as I was lugged up into the dark room in a cloud of smoke that made me gasp, holding out my hands to keep me from knocking against the sides of the trap, and not knowing whether to laugh at the foolishness of it all, or to cry at the sorrowfulness of this play-acting, which so mocked me. For here I was pretending to be the most beautiful woman that ever was, and a goddess into the bargain, and yet I was cursed as you know.

All was dimmery in the room. I could but just make out a figure at the far side. Beguildy was singing some queer kind of spell in the kitchen, and the young man's horse was stamping and shaking its bridle outside.

As I came up clear of the trap, and hung there in the rosy light, the young squire started forrard in his chair, and held out his hands like a child at a pastry shop. But I knew he was under solumn oath not to stir from his chair. I thought it must be a strange thing to go through life with men holding out their hands on this side and on that, to be always the pastry cake in the window with hungry eyes upon it. Then all of a sudden I heard a movement on the other side of the room, and turning that way I could have cried aloud, for there sat Kester Woodseaves.

Did ever Fate play such a trick? Here was the one man out of all the world that I must hide from, since already I loved him so dear, and so must never hurt him with my grief. And there he was, so close in the small place that two strides would have fetched him to me. He was leaning forrard like the young squire, and he made to hold his arms out and then drew back and gave a sigh, and I know now that the desire of woman was stirring within him. It came on me then with a great joy that it was my own self and no other that had made him hold out his arms. For in that place he could not see my curse, he could only see me gleaming pale as any woman would. Often since, I have wondered if he'd have been so stirred if it had been Jancis hanging there, crucified in nakedness, instead of me. Was it all of the flesh, as it was with the young squire, or did my soul, that was twin to his, draw him and wile him, succour his heart and summon his love, even, then? For I do think that the spirit makes herself busy about the body, and breathes through it, and throws a veil over it to make it more fair than it is of itself. For what is flesh alone? You may see flesh alone and feel nought but loathing. You may see it in the butcher's shop cut up, or in the gutter, drunken, or in the coffin, dead. For the world is full of flesh as the chandler's shelf is full of lanthorns at the beginning of winter. But it inna till you take the lanthorn home and light it that you have any comfort of it. And I have ever seen that the women with fair mounded cheeks, and breasts like the round pyatt where Felena danced, yet lacking any soul to laugh or weep in them, be not the ones that draw men. The ones that lure men to them by the tuthree, the score, and the hundred, as folk draw towards a lighted church, when the Easter Supper is ready, be often those that care not much for their bodies.

This is a strange thing, as true things are often, but not so strange as this wiling and summoning of a man by a woman flawed and cursed, a woman to whom it was said, 'You'll never have a lover.' Two men would have been my lovers that night if I'd willed it so. And as I saw the squire's shoulders stooped forrard with the weight of his longing I knew for the first time that, whatever my face might be, my body was fair enough. From foot to shoulder I was as passable as any woman could be. Under the red light my flesh was like rose petals, and the shape of me was such as the water-fairies were said to have, lissom and lovesome.

I hadna cared so much, nor been so dismayed, at playing this foolish game afore a stranger. But now I was all one blush from head to foot, and cold as ice as well. Every second was an hour, and I was shamed as if I had gone whoring. Yet I couldna but rejoice to have given my body in this wise to the eyes of him who was maister in the house of me for ever and ever.

I pulled the muslin over my face and looked slanting through it towards this wonder. For indeed he was a wonder to me then and always, not for his looks nor for anything that he did, but for the silent power of what he was, the power gathered up in him, as tremendous as a great mountain on the sky, that you couldna measure nor name, but only feel.

In the thinning smoke I could see him, with his face set beneath the shock of bodily love, for whether or not he loved me after, he did in that hour, and with the wounded look that is ever on the faces of men between the coming of the lust of the eye and its satisfying.

It takes a long while to write down, but I was only in the room as long as Missis Beguildy could count sixty. Beguildy was afraid they'd find him out if he allowed them too long, never dreaming, poor simple fool, that neither of them believed a word of his tales. While I was still faintly from the shock of seeing Kester Woodseaves, Beguildy called from the kitchen –

'Well, well, gentlemen, have I yearned my five pound?'

'Aye, aye!' says Mister Camperdine, with his look heavy on me, 'and more, and more!'

Beguildy began to sing another foolish rhyme, which was the sign for me to be ready to go down. Never was any woman so glad of a cellar as I was when I raught back there. I got into my clothes as quick as might be, for we could hear the squire argufying with Beguildy in the kitchen.

'What now? What now? Speak with a body?' Beguildy was saying. 'Now how can ye speak with Missis Venus, and she dead and gone this thousand year? I fetched her back for ye, through the grave and gate of death, for five pound in cash, but I canna keep her. She comes a-walking on the air, in a cloud, for the time you can count sixty, and then she's gone. For she is but a beautiful bogy, seesta! and she mun be raught home by candle-light.'

There was a great burst of laughter at that, and as Mister Camperdine went out to his horse, he called back –

'I'll have another look at Venus one day, Beguildy. She's got a very tidy figure, by Gad, *wherever* she's from!'

Mary Webb (1881–1927)

Ideas for discussion

■ The experience of being 'Venus' has a profound effect on Prue. In your group, discuss what this effect is and why taking part in what is, after all, a rather shabby trick should change her life. Here are some questions to help you:

- Is the raising of Venus merely a pornographic show?

- Why is it only when Prue sees Kester that she is ashamed?

- Why is it so important to Prue that her body should be desired?

- Why does she insist that Kester's love is not simply for her 'flesh'?

- Does Kester see Prue, or only the body of an unknown woman?

- How would you describe Prue's mood at the end of the passage?

■ Prue says, 'I thought it must be a strange thing to go through life with men holding out their hands on this side and on that, to be always the pastry cake in the window with hungry eyes upon it.' What does the passage as a whole say about the way in which men see women?

■ How does Mary Webb provide Prue with an individual voice? Discuss the use of dialect in the passage. Do you think that the language adds to its effectiveness?

Suggestions for writing

1 Use the ideas raised in your discussions to write about Raising Venus. You should discuss the characterisation, themes and language of the passage.

2 Write a story of your own in which someone who is never noticed by the opposite sex undergoes an experience similar to Prue's which changes her or his life. One example might be to update the idea by setting it during the school play. Costume and lighting can provide the necessary transformation. (Remember that posing as Venus allows Prue to appear before the men in disguise, and that her nakedness provides a kind of anonymity.)

  Tell the story through the main character's eyes.

3 Try writing a short piece in the local dialect of your area. If you decide on the kind of character who might speak in this way and just let her or him speak, you may find that you end up with a story.

unit 3

A world away

Since the beginning of time, people have always been fascinated by travellers' tales. This unit brings together three very different travel writers from a golden age of travel writing – the nineteenth century.

• A Camp-meeting•

In 1827, Mrs Frances Trollope, 48 years old and broke, set sail for America in the hope of reviving her fortunes. After various reckless and unsuccessful attempts at making money (including involving her son in a fake circus act and building the first shopping mall in Cincinnati), she decided to write a book about her American travels. *Domestic Manners of the Americans* proved to be an immediate bestseller.

Religious zeal has always been popular in America. In this extract, Trollope visits a camp-meeting of religious revivalists, and her English reserve is rather shaken by the display of such fervour.

At midnight a horn sounded through the camp, which, we were told, was to call the people from private to public worship; and we presently saw them flocking from all sides to the front of the preachers' stand. Mrs B—— and I contrived to place ourselves with our backs supported against the lower part of this structure, and we were thus enabled to witness the scene which followed, without personal danger. There were about two thousand persons assembled.

One of the preachers began in a low nasal tone, and, like all other Methodist preachers, assured us of the enormous depravity of man as he comes from the hands of his Maker, and of his perfect sanctification after he had wrestled sufficiently with the Lord to get hold of him, *et cetera*. The admiration of the crowd was evinced by almost constant cries of 'Amen! Amen!', 'Jesus! Jesus!', 'Glory! Glory!' and the like. But this comparative tranquillity did not last long; the preacher told them that 'this night was the time fixed upon for anxious sinners to wrestle with the Lord'; that he and his brethren 'were at hand to help them'; and that such as needed their help were to come forward into 'the pen' [...] 'The pen' was the space immediately below the preacher's stand; we were therefore placed on the edge of it, and were enabled to see and hear all that took place in the very centre of this extraordinary exhibition.

The crowd fell back at the mention of the *pen*, and for some minutes there was a vacant space before us. The preachers came down from their stand, and placed themselves in the midst of it, beginning to sing a hymn, calling upon the penitents to come forth. As they sang they kept turning themselves round to every part of the crowd, and, by degrees, the voices of the whole multitude joined in chorus. This was the only moment at which I perceived any thing like the solemn and beautiful effect which I had heard ascribed to this woodland worship. It is certain that the combined voices of such a multitude heard at dead of night, from the depths of their eternal forests, the many fair young faces turned upward, and looking paler and lovelier as they met the moonbeams, the dark figures of the officials in the middle of the circle, the lurid glare thrown by the altar-fires on the woods beyond, did altogether produce a fine and solemn effect, that I shall not easily forget; but ere I had well enjoyed it, the scene changed, and sublimity gave place to horror and disgust.

The exhortation nearly resembled that which I had heard at 'the Revival', but the result was very different; for, instead of the few hysterical women who had distinguished themselves on that occasion, above a hundred persons, nearly all females, came forward, uttering howlings and groans so terrible that I shall never cease to shudder when I recall them. They appeared to drag each other forward, and, on the word being given 'Let us pray', they all fell on their knees; but this posture was soon changed for others that permitted greater scope for the convulsive movements of their limbs; and they were soon all lying on the ground in an indescribable confusion of heads and legs. They threw about their limbs with such incessant and violent motion, that I was every instant expecting some serious accident to occur.

But how am I to describe the sounds that proceeded from this strange mass of human beings? I know no words which can convey an idea of it. Hysterical sobbings, convulsive groans, shrieks and screams the most appalling, burst forth on all sides. I felt sick with horror. As if their hoarse and overstrained voices failed to make noise enough, they soon began to clap their hands violently [. . .]

Many of these wretched creatures were beautiful young females. The preachers moved about among them, at once exciting and soothing their agonies. I heard the muttered 'Sister! dear sister!' I saw the insidious lips approach the cheeks of the unhappy girls; I heard the murmured confessions of the poor victims, and I watched their tormentors, breathing into their ears consolations that tinged the pale cheek with red. Had I been a man, I am sure I should have been guilty of some rash act of interference; nor do I believe that such a scene could have been acted in the presence of Englishmen without instant punishment being inflicted; not to mention the salutary discipline of the treadmill, which, beyond all question, would, in England, have been applied to check so turbulent and so vicious a scene.

After the first wild burst that followed their prostration, the moanings, in many instances, became loudly articulate; and I then experienced a strange vibration between tragic and comic feeling.

A very pretty girl, who was kneeling in the attitude of Canova's Magdalene immediately before us, amongst an immense quantity of jargon, broke out thus: 'Woe! woe to the backsliders! hear it, hear it, Jesus! when I was fifteen my mother died, and I backslided, oh Jesus, I backslided! take me home to my mother, Jesus! take me home to her, for I am weary! Oh John Mitchel! John Mitchel!' and after sobbing piteously behind her raised hands, she lifted her sweet face again, which was as pale as death, and said: 'Shall I sit on the sunny bank of salvation with my mother? my own dear mother? oh Jesus, take me home, take me home!'

Who could refuse a tear to this earnest wish for death in one so young and so lovely? But I saw her, ere I left the ground, with her hand fast locked, and her head supported by a man who looked very much as Don Juan might, when sent back to earth as too bad for the regions below.

One woman near us continued to 'call on the Lord', as it is termed, in the loudest possible tone, and without a moment's interval, for the two hours that we kept our dreadful station. She became frightfully hoarse, and her face so red as to make me expect she would burst a blood-vessel. Among the rest of her rant, she said: 'I will hold fast to Jesus, I never will let him go; if they take me to hell, I will still hold him fast, fast, fast!'

The stunning noise was sometimes varied by the preachers beginning to sing; but the convulsive movements of the poor maniacs only became more violent. At length the atrocious wickedness of this horrible scene increased to a degree of grossness, that drove us from our station: we returned to the carriage at about three o'clock in the morning, and passed the remainder of the night in listening to the ever increasing tumult at the pen. To sleep was impossible. At day-break the horn again sounded, to send them to private devotion; and in about an hour afterwards I saw the whole camp as joyously and eagerly employed in preparing and devouring their most substantial breakfasts as if the night had been passed in dancing; and I marked many a fair but pale face, that I recognised as a demoniac of the night, simpering beside a swain, to whom she carefully administered hot coffee and eggs. The preaching saint and the howling sinner seemed alike to relish this mode of recruiting their strength.

After enjoying abundance of strong tea, which proved a delightful restorative after a night so strangely spent, I wandered alone into the forest, and I never remember to have found perfect quiet more delightful.

We soon after left the ground; but before our departure we learnt that a very *satisfactory* collection had been made by the preachers, for Bibles, tracts, and *all other religious purposes*.

Frances Trollope (1780–1863)

Ideas for discussion

■ How would you describe Mrs Trollope's attitude to the events that she witnesses? Pick out some phrases that most clearly indicate her feelings.

■ How would one of the participants defend her or his behaviour at the camp? Here are some questions to help your discussion:

- Is the camp intended for spectators or participants?

- Is there any indication that the worshippers are faking their religious fervour?

- Do the worshippers seem at all self-conscious?

■ How do you feel about extreme religious belief? Do you find it easy to accept, or does it make you feel uncomfortable?

Suggestions for writing

Write a story in which a young man or woman becomes involved with an extreme religious sect. How does it affect his or her parents and friends? Is it just a phase, or is it the beginning of a new life?

(If this idea interests you, you might like to read *Invisible Friends* by Alison Lurie, *The Razor's Edge* by W. Somerset Maugham or *How I Became a Holy Mother* by Ruth Prawer Jhabvala, which all deal very effectively with this subject.)

• Cairo and the Plague •

In 1835, at the age of 26, Alexander Kinglake began his journey to the East. When he returned he wrote *Eothen*, an account of his travels. It became one of the most famous travel books ever written.

   In this extract, Kinglake has arrived in Cairo and is in search of a banker for whom he has a letter of introduction that will allow him to cash a cheque. However, another visitor has taken up residence in Cairo — the plague.

Very soon after my arrival I found out the abode of the Levantine to whom my credentials were addressed. At his door several persons (all Arabs) were hanging about and keeping guard. It was not till after some delay and the interchange of some communications with those in the interior of the citadel that I was admitted. At length, however, I was conducted through the court, and up a flight of stairs, and finally into the apartment where business was transacted. The room was divided by a good substantial fence of iron bars, and behind these defences the banker had his station. The truth was that from fear of the plague he had adopted the course usually taken by European residents, and had shut himself up 'in strict quarantine', – that is to say, that he had, as he hoped, cut himself off from all communication with infecting substances. The Europeans long resident in the East without any, or with scarcely any exception, are firmly convinced that the plague is propagated by contact, and by contact only – that if they can but avoid the touch of an infecting substance, they are safe, and that if they cannot, they die. This belief induces them to adopt the contrivance of putting themselves in that stage of seige which they call 'quarantine'. It is a part of their faith that metals and hempen ropes, and also, I fancy, one or two other substances, will not carry the infection: and they likewise believe that the germ of pestilence lying in an infected substance may be destroyed by submersion in water, or by the action of smoke. They therefore guard the doors of their houses with the utmost care against intrusion, and condemn themselves, with all the members of their family, including European servants, to a strict imprisonment within the walls of their dwelling. Their native attendants are not allowed to enter at all, but they make the necessary purchases of provisions: these are hauled up through one of the windows by means of a rope, and are afterwards soaked in water.

I knew nothing of these mysteries, and was not therefore prepared for the sort of reception I met with. I advanced to the iron fence, and putting my letter between the bars, politely proferred it to Mr Banker. Mr Banker received me with a sad and dejected look, and not 'with open arms,' or with any arms at all, but with – a pair of tongs! I placed my letters between the iron fingers: these instantly picked it up as it were a viper, and conveyed it away to be scorched and purified by fire and smoke. I was disgusted at this reception, and that the idea that anything of mine could carry infection to the poor wretch who stood on the other side of the bars – pale and trembling, and already meet for death. I looked with something of the Mahometan's feeling upon these little contrivances for eluding fate: and in this instance at least they were vain: a little while and the poor money-changer who had strived to guard the days of his life (as though they were coins) with bolts and bars of iron – he was seized by the plague, and he died [. . .]

By some happy perverseness (occasioned perhaps by my disgust at the notion of being received with a pair of tongs) I took it into my pleasant head that all the European notions about contagion were thoroughly unfounded – that the plague might be providential or 'epidemic' (as they phrase it), but was not contagious, and that I could not be killed by the touch of a woman's sleeve, nor yet by her blessed breath. I therefore determined that the plague should not alter my habits and amusements in any one respect. Though I came to this resolve from impulse, I think that I took the course which was in effect the most prudent, for the cheerfulness of spirits which I was thus enabled to retain discouraged the yellow-winged angel, and prevented him from taking a shot at me. I however so far respected the opinion of the Europeans that I avoided touching when I could do so without privation or inconvenience. This endeavour furnished me with a sort of amusement as I passed through the streets. The usual mode of moving from place to place in the city of Cairo is upon donkeys; of these great numbers are always in readiness, with donkey-boys attached. I had two who constantly (until one of them died of the plague) waited at my door upon the chance of being wanted. I found this way of moving about exceedingly pleasant, and never attempted any other. I had only to mount my beast, and tell my donkey-boy the point for which I was bound, and instantly I began to glide on at a capital pace. The streets of Cairo are not paved in any way, but strewed with a dry sandy soil so deadening to sound, that the footfall of my donkey could scarcely be heard. There is no *trottoir*, and as you ride through the streets you mingle with the people on foot: those who are in your way, upon being warned by the shouts of the donkey-boy, move very slightly aside so as to leave you a narrow lane for your passage. Through this you move at a gallop, gliding on delightfully in the very midst of crowds without being inconvenienced or stopped for a moment; it seems to you that it is not the donkey but the donkey-boy who wafts you along with his shouts through the pleasant groups, and air that comes thick with the fragrance of burial spice. 'Eh! Sheik, – Eh! Bint, – reggalek, – shumalek, etc., etc. – O old man, O virgin, get out of the way on the right – O Virgin, O old man, get out of the way on the left, –

this Englishman comes, he comes, he comes!' The narrow alley which these shouts cleared for my passage made it possible, though difficult, to go on for a long way without touching a single person, and my endeavours to avoid such contact were a sort of game for me in my loneliness. If I got through a street without being touched, I won; if I was touched, I lost – lost a deuce of a stake according to the theory of the Europeans; but that I deemed to be all nonsense – I only lost that game, and would certainly win the next [. . .]

Although the plague was now spreading quick and terrible havoc [. . .] I did not see very plainly any corresponding change in the looks of the streets until the seventh day after my arrival: I then first observed that the city was *silenced*. There were no outward signs of despair nor of violent terror, but many of the voices that had swelled the busy hum of men were already hushed in death, and the survivors, so used to scream and screech in their earnestness whenever they bought or sold, now showed an unwonted indifference about the affairs of this world: it was less worth while for men to haggle and haggle, and crack the sky with noisy bargains, when the Great Commander was there who could 'pay all their debts with the roll of his drum.'

At this time I was informed that of 25,000 people at Alexandria, 12,000 had died already; the Destroyer had come rather later to Cairo, but there was nothing of weariness in his strides. The deaths came faster than ever they befell in the plague of London: but the calmness of orientals under such visitations, and their habit of using biers for interment instead of burying coffins along with the bodies, rendered it practicable to dispose of the dead in the usual way, without shocking the people by any unaccustomed spectacle of horror. There was no tumbling of bodies into carts as in the plague of Florence and the plague of London; every man according to his station, was properly buried, and that in the accustomed way, except that he went to his grave at a pace more than usually rapid.

The funerals pouring through the streets were not the only public evidence of deaths. In Cairo this custom prevails: At the instant of a man's death (if his property is sufficient to justify the expense) professional howlers are employed. I believe that these persons are brought near to the dying man when his end appears to be approaching, and the moment that life is gone they lift up their voices and send forth a loud wail from the chamber of death. Thus I knew when my near neighbours died: sometimes the howls were near, sometimes more distant. Once I was awakened in the night by the wail of death in the next house, and another time by a like howl from the house opposite; and there were two or three minutes, I recollect, during which the howl seemed to be actually *running* along the street.

I happened to be rather teased at this time by a sore throat, and I thought it would be well to get it cured if I could before I again started on my travels. I therefore inquired for a Frank doctor, and was informed that the only one then at Cairo was a Bolognese refugee, a very young practitioner, and so poor that he had not been able to take flight as the other medical men had done. At such a time as this it was out of the question to *send* for a European physician; a person thus summoned would be sure to suppose that the patient was ill of the plague and would decline to come. I therefore rode to the young doctor's residence, ascended a flight or two of stairs, and knocked at his door. No one came immediately, but after some little delay the medico himself opened the door and admitted me. I of course made him understand that I had come to consult him, but before entering upon my throat grievance, I accepted a chair, and exchanged a sentence or two of commonplace conversation. Now the natural commonplace of the city at this season was of a gloomy sort – 'Come va la peste?' (how goes the plague?), and this was precisely the question I put. A deep sigh, and the words, 'Sette cento per giorno, signor' (seven hundred a day), pronounced in a tone of deepest sadness and dejection, were the answer I received. The day was not oppressively hot, yet I saw that the doctor was transpiring profusely, and even the outside surface of the thick shawl dressing-gown in which he had wrapped himself appeared to be moist. He was a handsome, pleasant-looking young fellow, but the deep melancholy of his tone did not tempt me to prolong the conversation, and without further delay I requested that my throat might be looked at. The medico held my chin in the usual way, and examined my throat; he then wrote me a prescription, and almost immediately afterwards I bade him farewell, but as he conducted me towards the door, I observed an expression of strange and unhappy watchfulness in his rolling eyes. It was not the next day, but the next day but one, if I rightly remember, that I sent to request another interview with my doctor. In due time Dthemetri, my messenger, returned looking sadly aghast. He had '*met* the medico,' for so he phrased it, 'coming out from his house – in a bier!'

Alexander Kinglake (1809–1891)

Ideas for discussion

- There are no graphic descriptions of the dead and dying. How does Kinglake convey the horror of the plague?

- Despite its grisly subject matter there is a comic quality to much of the writing in this passage. Why do you think this is?

Suggestions for writing

This passage tells us a great deal about the way different people react to physical danger. The author, the Levantine banker and the Italian doctor all react in different ways. Write a story of your own in which a group of people have to face up to danger. Show how each character reacts in his or her own way. Here are some ideas to help you:

- A school party is held hostage by terrorists.

- A building society is held up by armed raiders. The police arrive and surround the building, but the gunmen refuse to come out.

- A modern city is infected with a new plague. Some survivors decide to escape to the country.

(You might like to read *After the First Death* by Robert Cormier, *The Siege of Babylon* by Farrukh Dhondy, *The Devil's Children* by Peter Dickinson, *The Plague* by Albert Camus or *A Journal of the Plague Year* by Daniel Defoe, which deal with the way that people cope with violence and death.)

Trailing-the-enemy and his wife, of the Kiowa tribe.

• Meeting the white man •

Towards the end of the nineteenth century, Buffalo Child Long Lance became chief of the Blackfoot tribe of the north-west of the United States. In his memoirs he tells of his first meeting as a young boy with the white man.

We travelled along the Namaka until we came to the foothills of the Rockies, and here we came upon the Suksiseoketuk Indians – the Rocky Mountain Band of Assiniboines – whose hunting-grounds were up there in the foothill country. Their chief, Chief Travels-Against-The-Wind, asked us who we were. Our chief said:

'We are roving *Seeha-sapa* from the plains, whose only enemy is the *Okotoks Isahpo* – the Rock Band of Crows.'

'*Ha-h! Neena-washtay – washtaydo. Amba wastaytch, See-ha-sapa*! – Oh! Very good – exceptionally good. Howdy do Blackfeet,' said the Suksiseoketuk chief.

Then he told our chief to tell his tribesmen to get off their ponies and sit down and he would have the Suksiseoketuk women make us some of the white man's *minne-seeha* – 'black water', or tea. And the chief said that while we were drinking of it he would tell us about the white man.

We had never had tea before, and we youngsters did not like it; it was bitter. The chief said that the Hudson's Bay Company had traded it for some of their skins – and they seemed to like this tea. Our old people liked it, too.

But we boys were very interested in what the chief told us about the white man. He told us to beware of his food; as it would make our teeth come out. He told us about the bread and the sweets which the white man ate, and he pulled up his upper lip and said:

'*Wambadahka* – Behold – my teeth are good, and so are the teeth of all our old people; but behold,' he said, walking over to a young boy and pulling up his lip, 'behold, these teeth of the young people are not good – too much white man's food. Our people, like yours, never used to die until they were over a hundred years old. Now, since we started to eat that white man's food we are sick all of the time. We keep getting worse and soon it will kill us all.'

And then the chief reached up and took hold of a shock of his hair at the top of his head, and he said:

'*Payheeh* – hair – the white man has none of this on top of his head. The crown of his head is as slick as the nose of a buffalo. Every time the Indian eats he wipes grease into his hair. White man wash it all out with bad medicine – soap – take all grease out and make all of his hair drop off. Swap your buffalo robes for the white man's blankets and gunpowder, but take not of his food,' said the chief, 'nor of his "bad medicine" for washing your hair.'

The next day we started north, accompanied by fifty of the Suksiseoketuk warriors. We travelled for six days, keeping always to the edge of the foothills. On the sixth day the Suksiseoketuks told us to pitch our camp at a point we had reached late in the afternoon, and they would send over a messenger to tell the white people at the trading post that we were there to see them.

After we had pitched our camp, several of our warriors went out to see if they could find some otter, which were plentiful in that part of the northland. While they were out they came upon a cabin, and they saw six long-haired people with light skin, going in and out of this place. Our warriors sat down and watched them and tried to figure out what they were; they had never seen any people like them before. They were not Indians and they were not white men; so one of our warriors, Big Darkness, said that they must be the white man's woman – their wives – white women! They had never seen any white women before; so they all agreed that that must be what they were.

But when they came back to camp and told the others about it, another of our warriors, Sun Calf, who had seen the women, changed his mind and said that he did not believe they were white women after all; they were 'some other kind of people', he said.

This started an argument which became so heated that our chief was afraid that it would lead to a fight. So he said the best way to settle the dispute was for the two warriors to put up a bet, and then go over and capture one of the 'strange beings' and bring it back, and the camp would decide what they were.

The men led out five ponies each and bet them on their respective beliefs. And when darkness came ten of our warriors, including Big Darkness and Sun Calf, crept over to the shack and overpowered one of the 'strange beings' and brought it back.

When they returned to our camp, we were waiting around a big fire singing, so that the disturbance would not attract the trading post. They led a very scared-looking 'being' to the edge of the fire, and Big Darkness exclaimed to the throng:

'Now look. Is it not a woman?'

Half of the tribe believed that it was a woman, and the other half said that it was not. The confusion of the argument which followed grew so noisy that it awoke some of the Suksiseoketuk warriors who had their camp about a hundred yards away, and they came over to see what was going on.

They stopped and listened for a moment, and then they began to laugh. They laughed for a long time before they would tell us what they were laughing at. And then one of them said:

'Inexperienced Blackfeet! It is neither a white woman nor any kind of being that you have ever seen before. It is a man from across the *Minne-Tonka*,' and he waved his arm towards the Pacific Ocean.

It was a Chinaman! One of the Chinese employed as cooks by some white prospectors.

Chief Buffalo Child Long Lance

Ideas for discussion

■ What impression do you get of the effect the white man had on the lives of the Indians?

- Do they seem afraid of white men?

- Do they hate them?

- Are they interested in them?

Suggestions for writing

Write a version of this event from the point of view of the Chinese cook. What image of Indians might he have received from the prospectors? How would he feel as he was grabbed and dragged to the camp to be stared at by a group of squabbling Indians?

unit 4

The wall is strong

This unit deals with one of the most fundamental human desires — the desire for freedom. It begins with a group of four poems on the subject of captivity and freedom, and continues with a collection of poetry and prose in which writers expose the injustices of their societies.

Freedom lost and found

Three of the following poems examine the feelings of prisoners. The final poem celebrates freedom.

In 1895, at the height of his popularity, Oscar Wilde was accused of being a 'posing sodomite', and, after a series of trials, was sentenced to two years' hard labour for homosexual offences. After his release, he wrote his most famous poem, 'The Ballad of Reading Gaol'. He died in 1900.

from *The Ballad of Reading Gaol*

V

I know not whether Laws be right,
    Or whether Laws be wrong;
All that we know who lie in gaol
    Is that the wall is strong;
And that each day is like a year,
    A year whose days are long.

But this I know, that every Law
    That men have made for Man,
Since first Man took his brother's life,
    And the sad world began,
But straws the wheat and saves the chaff
    With a most evil fan.

This too I know – and wise it were
    If each could know the same –
That every prison that men build
    Is built with bricks of shame,
And bound with bars lest Christ should see
    How men their brothers maim.

With bars they blur the gracious moon,
    And blind the goodly sun:
And they do well to hide their Hell,
    For in it things are done
That Son of God nor son of Man
    Ever should look upon!

*

The vilest deeds like poison weeds
    Bloom well in prison-air:
It is only what is good in Man
    That wastes and withers there:
Pale Anguish keeps the heavy gate,
    And the Warder is Despair.

For they starve the little frightened child
    Till it weeps both night and day:
And they scourge the weak, and flog the fool,
    And gibe the old and gray,
And some grow mad, and all grow bad,
    And none a word may say.

Each narrow cell in which we dwell
    Is a foul and dark latrine,
And the fetid breath of living Death
    Chokes up each grated screen,
And all, but Lust, is turned to dust
    In Humanity's machine.

The brackish water that we drink
    Creeps with a loathsome slime,
And the bitter bread they weigh in scales
    Is full of chalk and lime,
And Sleep will not lie down, but walks
    Wild-eyed, and cries to Time.

*

But though lean Hunger and green Thirst
  Like asp with adder fight,
We have little care of prison fare,
  For what chills and kills outright
Is that every stone one lifts by day
  Becomes one's heart at night.

With midnight always in one's heart,
  And twilight in one's cell,
We turn the crank, or tear the rope,
  Each in his separate Hell,
And the silence is more awful far
  Than the sound of brazen bell.

And never a human voice comes near
  To speak a gentle word:
And the eye that watches through the door
  Is pitiless and hard:
And by all forgot, we rot and rot,
  With soul and body marred.

And thus we rust Life's iron chain
  Degraded and alone:
And some men curse, and some men weep,
  And some men make no moan:
But God's eternal Laws are kind
  And break the heart of stone.

Oscar Wilde (1854–1900)

John Clare spent many years in lunatic asylums, suffering from what we would now diagnose as severe depression. He nevertheless continued to write some of the finest lyric poetry in the English language.

Written in Northampton County Asylum

I am! yet what I am who cares, or knows?
  My friends forsake me like a memory lost.
I am the self-consumer of my woes;
  They rise and vanish, an oblivious host,
Shadows of life, whose very soul is lost.
And yet I am – I live – though I am toss'd

Into the nothingness of scorn and noise,
  Into the living sea of waking dream,
Where there is neither sense of life, nor joys,
  But the huge shipwreck of my own esteem
And all that's dear. Even those I loved the best
Are strange – nay, they are stranger than the rest.

I long for scenes where man has never trod –
  For scenes where woman never smiled or wept –
There to abide with my Creator, God,
  And sleep as I in childhood sweetly slept,
Full of high thoughts, unborn. So let me lie, –
The grass below; above, the vaulted sky.

John Clare (1793–1864)

In his lifetime, Rudyard Kipling was one of the most popular poets in the English language. This poem comes from a series called 'The Barrack-Room Ballads', in which he gave voice to the thoughts and feelings of the ordinary British soldier during the Boer War.

Chant-Pagan

ENGLISH IRREGULAR: '99–02

Me that 'ave been what I've been,
Me that 'ave gone where I've gone,
Me that 'ave seen what I've seen –
   'Ow can I ever take on
With awful old England again,
An' 'ouses both sides of the street,
And 'edges two sides of the lane,
And the parson an' 'gentry' between,
An' touchin' my 'at when we meet –
   Me that 'ave been what I've been?

Me that 'ave watched 'arf a world
'Eave up all shiny with dew,
Kopje on kop to the sun,
An' as soon as the mist let 'em through
Our 'elios winkin' like fun –
Three sides of a ninety-mile square,
Over valleys as big as a shire –
Are ye there? Are ye there? Are ye there?
An' then the blind drum of our fire . . .
An' I'm rollin' 'is lawns for the Squire,
Me!

Me that 'ave rode through the dark
Forty mile often on end,
Along the Ma'ollisberg Range,
With only the stars for my mark
An' only the night for my friend,
An' things runnin' off as you pass,
An' things jumpin' up in the grass,
An' the silence, the shine an' the size
Of the 'igh, inexpressible skies. . .
I am takin' some letters almost
As much as a mile, to the post,
An' 'mind you come back with the change!'
Me!

Me that saw Barberton took
When we dropped through the clouds on their 'ead,
An' they 'ove the guns over and fled –
Me that was through Di'mond 'Ill,
An' Pieters an' Springs an' Belfast –
From Dundee to Vereeniging all!
Me that stuck out to the last
(An' five bloomin' bars on my chest) –
I am doin' my Sunday-school best,
By the 'elp of the Squire an' 'is wife
(Not to mention the 'ousemaid an' cook),
To come in an' 'ands up an' be still,
An' honestly work for my bread,
My livin' in that state of life
To which it shall please God to call
Me!

Me that 'ave followed my trade
In the place where the lightnin's are made,
'Twixt the Rains and the Sun and the Moon;
Me that lay down an' got up
Three years an' the sky for my roof –
That 'ave ridden my 'unger an' thirst
Six thousand raw mile on the hoof,
With the Vaal and the Orange for cup,
An' the Brandwater Basin for dish, –
Oh! it's 'ard to be'ave as they wish,
(Too 'ard, an' a little too soon),
I'll 'ave to think over it first –

                            Me!

I will arise an' get 'ence; –
I will trek South and make sure
If it's only my fancy or not
That the sunshine of England is pale.
And the breezes of England are stale,
An' there's somethin' gone small with the lot;
For *I* know of a sun an' a wind,
An' some plains and a mountain be'ind,
An' some graves by a barb-wire fence;
An' a Dutchman I've fought 'oo might give
Me a job were I ever inclined,
To look in an' offsaddle an' live
Where there's neither a road nor a tree –
But only my Maker an' me,
And I think it will kill me or cure,
So I think I will go there an' see.

Rudyard Kipling (1865–1936)

Walt Whitman wrote one of the great celebrations of America in his long poem sequence 'Leaves of Grass', from which this poem is taken.

I Hear America Singing

I hear America singing, the varied carols I hear,
Those of mechanics, each one singing his as it should be blithe and strong,
The carpenter singing his as he measures his plank or beam,
The mason singing his as he makes ready for work, or leaves off work,
The boatman singing what belongs to him in his boat, the deck-hand singing
    on the steamboat deck,
The shoemaker singing as he sits on his bench, the hatter singing as he stands,
The wood-cutter's song, the ploughboy's on his way in the morning, or at
    noon intermission or at sundown,
The delicious singing of the mother, or of the young wife at work, or of the
    girl sewing or washing,
Each singing what belongs to him or her and to none else,
The day what belongs to the day – at night the party of young fellows,
    robust, friendly,
Singing with open mouths their strong melodious songs.

Walt Whitman (1819–1892)

Ideas for discussion

- Look closely at the first two poems. What does imprisonment mean to these poets? Does the fact that Wilde and Clare are writing from experience make a difference?

  How does each poet imagine freedom? Wilde does not actually describe freedom in this extract, but if you examine the poem closely you can work out how he *would* describe it.

- Oscar Wilde says quite clearly that prison is an evil institution. How convincing do you find his arguments?

- 'Chant-Pagan' describes a man imprisoned by society. Why do you think he feels so trapped?

- How does Walt Whitman convey a feeling of freedom in 'I Hear America Singing'? It might help you to compare the society he describes with the society presented in 'Chant-Pagan'.

Suggestions for writing

1 Compare the ways in which the four poems deal with freedom and captivity. Remember that each poet has chosen a particular form for his poem (for instance, there are two very different poems that call themselves ballads) and that this contributes to the poem's effectiveness.

2 Imagine that Oscar Wilde wrote a letter to a newspaper putting forward his arguments for the abolition of prisons. Write a version of this letter using the poem for guidance.

  (Wilde did in fact write a series of letters to *The Daily Chronicle* after his release.)

3 Imagine that, before he leaves for South Africa, the soldier of 'Chant-Pagan' decides to explain his decision to the squire. Write the scene that might take place. Tell the story from the point of view of the soldier.

  You could also write a companion piece in the form of the experiences of a contemporary soldier returned from service in a foreign war. Might he view modern Britain in the same way as the soldier in the poem?

4 Walt Whitman's poem is really a list of different kinds of Americans who seem to him happy and free. Could you write a similar piece celebrating the various occupations of modern Britain? What about the traffic warden or for that matter, the teacher? If you find it difficult to do this, think about *why* it is difficult.

  If you feel that you cannot write a serious version of Whitman's 'song' then try a parody.

The poor and the powerless

All the writers in this section were pioneers, in the sense that they were among the first to speak out about the injustices that they saw around them.

In Europe, until recently only a minority of the population could read, and so writers were generally writing for a small but highly educated readership. However, although they were academically educated, middle-class readers were often ignorant of the conditions of other sections of society. The writers in this section wanted to educate their readers.

This part of the unit begins with two famous writers, Charles Kingsley and William Makepeace Thackeray, telling their readers some unpleasant truths about the society in which they live.

• The Lowest Deep •

This extract is from Charles Kingsley's *Alton Locke*, published in 1850. The hero of the book, Alton Locke, is a cockney tailor and poet who becomes a trade union leader and is eventually sent to prison. In this episode, he meets an old friend who has fallen on hard times and Locke accompanies him to his tenement in the slums of Bermondsey.

> He stopped at the end of a miserable blind alley, where a dirty gas-lamp just served to make darkness visible, and show the patched windows and rickety doorways of the crazy houses, whose upper stories were lost in a brooding cloud of fog; and the pools of stagnant water at our feet; and the huge heap of cinders which filled up the waste end of the alley – a dreary black, formless mound, on which two or three spectral dogs prowled up and down after the offal, appearing and vanishing like dark imps in and out of the black misty chaos beyond.
>
> The neighbourhood was undergoing, as it seemed, 'improvements', of that peculiar metropolitan species which consists in pulling down the dwellings of the poor, and building up rich men's houses instead; and great buildings, within high temporary palings, had already eaten up half the little houses; as the great fish, and the great estates, and the great shop-keepers, eat up the little ones of their species – by the law of competition, lately discovered to be the true creator and preserver of the universe.

There they loomed up, the tall bullies, against the dreary sky, looking down with their grim, proud, bony visages, on the misery which they were driving out of one corner, only to accumulate and intensify it in another.

The house at which we stopped was the last in the row; all its companions had been pulled down; and there it stood, leaning out with one naked ugly side into the gap, and stretching out long props, like feeble arms and crutches, to resist the work of demolition.

A group of slatternly people were in the entry, talking loudly, and as Downes pushed by them, a woman seized him by the arm.

'Oh! you unnatural villain! – To go away after your drink, and leave all them poor dear dead corpses locked up, without even letting a body go in to stretch them out!'

'And breeding the fever, too, to poison the whole house!' growled one.

'The relieving officer's been here, my cove,' said another; 'and he's gone for a peeler and a search warrant to break open the door, I can tell you!'

But Downes pushed past unheeding, unlocked a door at the end of the passage, thrust me in, locked it again, and then rushed across the room in chase of two or three rats, who vanished into cracks and holes.

And what a room! A low lean-to with wooden walls, without a single article of furniture; and through the broad chinks of the floor shone up as it were ugly glaring eyes, staring at us. – They were the reflections of the rushlight in the sewer below. The stench was frightful – the air heavy with pestilence. The first breath I drew made my heart sink, and my stomach turn. But I forget everything in the object which lay before me, as Downes tore a half-finished coat off three corpses laid side by side on the bare floor.

There was his little Irish wife; – dead – and naked – the wasted white limbs gleamed in the lurid light; the unclosed eyes stared, as if reproachfully, at the husband whose drunkenness had brought her there to kill her with the pestilence; and on each side of her a little, shrivelled, impish, child-corpse – the wretched man had laid their arms round the dead mother's neck – and there they slept, their hungering and wailing over at last for ever: the rats had been busy already with them – but what matter to them now?

'Look!' he cried; 'I watched 'em dying! Day after day I saw the devils come up through the cracks, like little maggots and beetles, and all manner of ugly things, creeping down their throats; and I asked 'em, and they said they were the fever devils.'

It was too true; the poisonous exhalations had killed them. The wretched man's delirium tremens had given that horrible substantiality to the poisonous fever gases.

Suddenly Downes turned on me, almost menacingly. 'Money! money! I want some gin!'

I was thoroughly terrified – and there was no shame in feeling fear, locked up with a madman far my superior in size and strength, in so ghastly a place. But the shame, and the folly too, would have been in giving way to my fear; and with a boldness half assumed, half the real fruit of excitement and indignation at the horrors I beheld, I answered –

'If I had money, I would give you none. What do you want with gin? Look at the fruits of your accursed tippling. If you had taken my advice, my poor fellow,' I went on, gaining courage as I spoke, 'and become a water-drinker, like me – '

'Curse you and your water-drinking! If you had had no water to drink or wash with for two years but that – that', pointing to the foul ditch below – 'If you had emptied the slops in there with one hand, and filled your kettle with the other – '

'Do you actually mean that that sewer is your only drinking water?'

'Where else can we get any? Everybody drinks it; and you shall, too – you shall!' he cried, with a fearful oath, 'and then see if you don't run off to the gin-shop, to take the taste of it out of your mouth. Drink? and who can help drinking, with his stomach turned with such a hell-broth as that – or such a hell's blast as this air is here, ready to vomit from morning till night with the smells? I'll show you. You shall drink a bucket full of it, as sure as you live, you shall.'

And he ran out of the back door, upon a little balcony, which hung over the ditch.

I tried the door, but the key was gone, and the handle too. I beat furiously on it, and called for help. Two gruff authoritative voices were heard in the passage.

'Let us in; I'm the policeman!'

'Let me out, or mischief will happen!'

The policeman made a vigorous thrust at the crazy door; and just as it burst open, and the light of his lantern streamed into the horrible den, a heavy splash was heard outside.

'He has fallen into the ditch!'

'He'll be drowned, then, as sure as he's a born man,' shouted one of the crowd behind.

We rushed out on the balcony. The light of the policeman's lantern glared over the ghastly scene – along the double row of miserable house-backs, which lined the sides of the open tidal ditch – over strange rambling jetties, and balconies, and sleeping sheds, which hung on rotting piles over the black waters, with phosphorescent scraps of rotten fish gleaming and twinkling out of the dark hollows, like devilish grave-lights – over bubbles of poisonous gas, and bloated carcasses of dogs, and lumps of offal, floating on the stagnant olive-green hell-broth – over the slow sullen rows of oily ripple which were dying away into the darkness far beyond, sending up, as they stirred, hot breaths of miasma – the only sign that a spark of humanity, after years of foul life, had quenched itself at last in that foul death. I almost fancied that I could see the haggard face staring up at me through the slimy water; but no – it was as opaque as stone.

I shuddered and went in again, to see slatternly gin-smelling women stripping off their clothes – true women even there – to cover the poor naked corpses; and pointing to the bruises which told a tale of long tyranny and cruelty; and mingling their lamentations with stories of shrieks and beating, and children locked up for hours to starve; and the men looked on sullenly, as if they too were guilty, or rushed out to relieve themselves by helping to find the drowned body. Ugh! it was the very mouth of hell, that room. And in the midst of all the rout, the relieving officer stood impassive, jotting down scraps of information, and warning us to appear the next day, to state what we knew before the magistrates. Needless hypocrisy of law! Too careless to save the woman and children from brutal tyranny, nakedness, starvation! – Too superstitious to offend the idol of vested interests, by protecting the poor man against his tyrants, the house-owning shopkeepers under whose greed the dwellings of the poor become nests of filth and pestilence, drunkenness and degradation. Careless, superstitious, imbecile law! – leaving the victims to die unhelped, and then, when the fever and the tyranny has done its work, in thy sanctimonious prudishness, drugging thy respectable conscience by a 'searching inquiry' as to how it all happened – lest, forsooth, there should have been 'foul play!' Is the knife or the bludgeon, then, the only foul play, and not the cesspool and the curse of Rabshakeh? Go through Bermondsey or Spitalfields, St Giles's or Lambeth and see if *there* is not foul play enough already – to be tried hereafter at a more awful coroner's inquest than thou thinkst of!

Charles Kingsley (1819–1875)

Ideas for discussion

■ Charles Kingsley was a priest who, after the publication of *Alton Locke*, was banned from preaching by the Bishop of London. Are there any passages in this extract that seem like examples of preaching? What makes them sound that way?

■ What do you think was Kingsley's purpose in including an episode like this in a novel which, after all, is meant to be a piece of fiction? If he wanted to change the law, would he not have done better to write to a newspaper or publish a pamphlet?

● Waiting at the Station ●

The following article is taken from 'Sketches and Travels in London' and was originally published in *Punch* in 1850. Like Charles Kingsley, Thackeray was determined to tell his readers about another world – the world of the poor.

We are amongst a number of people waiting for the Blackwall train at the Fenchurch Street Station. Some of us are going a little farther than Blackwall – as far as Gravesend; some of us are going even farther than Gravesend – to Port Phillip in Australia, leaving behind the *patriae fines* and the pleasant fields of Old England. It is rather a queer sensation to be in the same boat and station with a party that is going upon so prodigious a journey. One speculates about them with more than an ordinary interest, thinking of the difference between your fate and theirs, and that we shall never behold these faces again.

Some eight-and-thirty women are sitting in the large Hall of the station, with bundles, baskets, and light baggage, waiting for the steamer, and the orders to embark. A few friends are taking leave of them, bonnets are laid together, and whispering going on. A little crying is taking place; – only a very little crying, –

and among those who remain, as it seems to me, not those who are going away. They leave behind them little to weep for; they are going from bitter cold and hunger, constant want and unavailing labour. Why should they be sorry to quit a mother who has been so hard to them as our country has been? How many of these women will ever see the shore again, upon the brink of which they stand, and from which they will depart in a few minutes more? It makes one sad and ashamed too, that they should not be more sorry. But how are you to expect love where you have given such scanty kindness? If you saw your children glad at the thoughts of leaving you, and for ever: would you blame yourselves or them? It is not that the children are ungrateful, but the home was unhappy, and the parents indifferent or unkind. You are in the wrong, under whose government they only had neglect and wretchedness; not they, who can't be called upon to love such an unlovely thing as misery, or to make any other return for neglect but indifference and aversion. [. . .]

If you go up and speak to one of these women, as you do, (and very good-naturedly, and you can't help that confounded condescension,) she curtsies and holds down her head meekly, and replies with modesty, as becomes her station, to your honour with the clean shirt and the well-made coat. 'And so she should,' is what hundreds of thousands of us, rich and poor, say still. Both believe this to be bounden duty; and that a poor person should naturally bob her head to a rich one physically and morally.

Let us get her last curtsey from her as she stands here upon the English shore. When she gets into the Australian woods her back won't bend except to her labour; or, if it do, from old habit and the reminiscence of the old country, do you suppose her children will be like that timid creature before you? They will know nothing of that Gothic society, with its ranks and hierarchies, its cumbrous ceremonies, its glittering antique paraphernalia, in which we have been educated; in which rich and poor still acquiesce, and which multitudes of both still admire: far removed from these old-world traditions, they will be bred up in the midst of plenty, freedom, manly brotherhood. Do you think if your worship's grandson goes into the Australian woods, or meets the grandchild of one of yonder women by the banks of the Warrawarra, the Australian will take a hat off or bob a curtsey to the new comer? He will hold out his hand, and say, 'Stranger, come into my house and take a shakedown, and have a share of our supper. You come out of the old country, do you? There was some people were kind to my grandmother there, and sent her out to Melbourne. Times are changed since then – come in and welcome!'

What a confession it is that we have almost all of us been obliged to make! A clever and earnest-minded writer gets a commission from the *Morning Chronicle* newspaper, and reports upon the state of our poor in London; he goes amongst labouring people and poor of all kinds – and brings back what? A picture of human life so wonderful, so awful, so piteous and pathetic, so exciting and terrible, that readers of romances own they never read anything like to it; and that the griefs, struggles, strange adventures here depicted, exceed anything that any of us could imagine. Yes; and these wonders and terrors have been lying by your door and mine ever since we had a door of our own. We had but to go a hundred yards off and see for ourselves, but we never did. Don't we pay poor-rates, and are they not heavy enough in the name of patience? Very true; and we have our own private pensioners, and give away some of our superfluity, very likely. You are not unkind; not ungenerous. But of such wondrous and complicated misery as this you confess you had no idea. No. How should you? – you and I – we are of the upper classes; we have had hitherto no community with the poor. We never speak a word to the servant who waits on us for twenty years; we condescend to employ a tradesman, keeping him at a proper distance, mind, of course, at a proper distance – we laugh at his young men, if they dance, jig, and amuse themselves like their betters, and call them counter-jumpers, snobs, and what not; of his workmen we know nothing, how pitilessly they are ground down, how they live and die, here close by us at the backs of our houses; until some poet like Hood wakes and sings that dreadful '*Song of the Shirt;*' some prophet like Carlyle rises up and denounces woe; some clear-sighted, energetic man like the writer of the *Chronicle* travels into the poor man's country for us, and comes back with his tale of terror and wonder.

Awful, awful poor man's country! The bell rings, and these eight-and-thirty women bid adieu to it, rescued from it (as a few thousands more will be) by some kind people who are interested in their behalf. In two hours more, the steamer lies alongside the ship *Culloden*, which will bear them to their new home. Here are the berths aft for the unmarried women, the married couples are in the midships, the bachelors in the fore-part of the ship. Above and below decks it swarms and echoes with the bustle of departure. The Emigration Commissioner comes and calls over their names; there are old and young, large families, numbers of

children already accustomed to the ship, and looking about with amused unconsciousness. One was born but just now on board; he will not know how to speak English till he is fifteen thousand miles away from home. Some of these kind people whose bounty and benevolence organized the Female Emigration Scheme, are here to give a last word and shake of the hand to their *protégées*. They hang sadly and gratefully round their patrons. One of them, a clergyman, who has devoted himself to this good work, says a few words to them at parting. It is a solemn minute indeed – for those who (with the few thousands who will follow them) are leaving the country and escaping from the question between rich and poor; and what for those who remain? But, at least, those who go will remember that in their misery here they found gentle hearts to love and pity them, and generous hands to give them succour, and will plant in the new country this grateful tradition of the old. – May heaven's good mercy speed them!

William Makepeace Thackeray (1811–1863)

Ideas for discussion

■ This article is not fictional. How does it compare with Kingsley's fictional view of the poor? Do you find them equally powerful?

■ What does a modern reader gain from reading this article?

■ There is a lot of talk nowadays about the importance of 'the classless society'. How different is modern society from the class-ridden society described by Thackeray?

■ Thackeray refers on p.108 to 'The poor man's country' as if it were a land unknown to his readers. Does such a place still exist?

■ How does Thackeray see Australia? Look carefully at the article and try to build up a picture of what Australia means to Thackeray.

Suggestions for writing

1 'The Lowest Deep' and 'Waiting at the Station' are both pieces of documentary writing which attempt to depict the life of the Victorian poor. It could be argued, therefore, that they are only of interest to historians. Do you think that there is a case for reading them in the 1990s? If so, write an essay in which you explain why you think such pieces ought to be read.

2 The nearest modern equivalent to the kind of deprivation highlighted by Kingsley and Thackeray is to be found amongst the homeless sleeping rough in the streets of our major cities. You may feel that people are ignoring this problem and that they need to be made more aware.

Devise a publicity campaign that draws attention to the plight of the homeless. You could include the following:

● a fictionalised diary of a young person sleeping rough

● a series of newspaper advertisements

● a pamphlet to be given out in shopping centres and high streets.

From slavery to freedom

The next two passages were written by black Americans and represent the earliest examples of books which deal with the realities of the black experience.

Frederick Douglass

• The White Man's Power •

The first extract comes from Frederick Douglass's account of his life as a slave in the southern states of America and his eventual flight to freedom in the north.

When Douglass escaped, he toured America lecturing on the evils of slavery and became famous as an orator. However, many pro-slavers could not believe that a former slave could so quickly become such an educated and articulate speaker, and they accused him of being a fraud. To combat these charges he wrote his autobiography which was published in 1845 along with a number of other slave autobiographies and did much to hasten the eventual abolition of slavery in America.

Douglass later became a bank president and ended his distinguished career as a diplomat.

My new mistress proved to be all she appeared when I first met her at the door, – a woman of the kindest heart and finest feelings. She had never had a slave under her control previously to myself, and prior to her marriage she had been dependent upon her own industry for a living. She was by trade a weaver; and by constant application to her business, she had been in a good degree preserved from the blighting and dehumanizing effects of slavery. I was utterly astonished at her goodness. I scarcely knew how to behave towards her. She was entirely unlike any other white woman I had ever seen. I could not approach her as I was accustomed to approach other white ladies. My early instruction was all out of place. The crouching servility, usually so acceptable a quality in a slave, did not answer when manifested toward her. Her favor was not gained by it; she seemed to be disturbed by it. She did not deem it impudent or unmannerly for a slave to look her in the face. The meanest slave was put fully at ease in her presence, and none left without feeling better for having seen her. Her face was made of heavenly smiles, and her voice of tranquil music.

But, alas! this kind heart had but a short time to remain such. The fatal poison of irresponsible power was already in her hands, and soon commenced its infernal work. That cheerful eye, under the influence of slavery, soon became red with rage; that voice, made all of sweet accord, changed to one of harsh and horrid discord; and that angelic face gave place to that of a demon.

Very soon after I went to live with Mr and Mrs Auld, she very kindly commenced to teach me the A, B, C. After I had learned this, she assisted me in learning to spell words of three or four letters. Just at this point of my progress, Mr Auld found out what was going on, and at once forbade Mrs Auld to instruct me further, telling her, among other things, that it was unlawful, as well as unsafe, to teach a slave to read. To use his own words, further, he said, 'If you give a nigger an inch, he will take an ell. A nigger should know nothing but to obey his master – to do as he is told to do. Learning would *spoil* the best nigger in the world. Now,' said he, 'if you teach that nigger (speaking of myself) how to read, there would be no keeping him. It would forever unfit him to be a slave. He would at once become unmanageable, and of no value to his master. As to himself, it could do him no good, but a great deal of harm. It would make him discontented and unhappy.' These words sank deep into my heart, stirred up sentiments within that lay slumbering, and called into existence an entirely new train of thought. It was a new and special revelation, explaining dark and mysterious things, with which my youthful understanding had struggled, but struggled in vain. I now understood what had been to me a most perplexing difficulty – to wit, the white man's power to enslave the black man. It was a grand achievement, and I prized it highly. From that moment, I understood the pathway from slavery to freedom. It was just what I wanted, and I got it at a time when I the least expected it. Whilst I was saddened by the thought of losing the aid of my kind mistress, I was gladdened by the invaluable instruction which, by the merest accident, I had gained from my master. Though conscious of the difficulty of learning without a teacher, I set out with high hope, and a fixed purpose, at whatever cost of trouble, to learn how to read. The very decided manner with which he spoke, and strove to impress his wife with the evil consequences of giving me instruction, served to convince me that he was deeply sensible of the truths he was uttering. It gave me the best assurance that I might rely with the utmost confidence on the results which, he said, would flow from teaching me to read. What he most dreaded, that I most desired. What he most loved, that I most hated. That which to him was a great evil, to be carefully shunned, was to me a great good, to be diligently sought; and the argument which he so warmly urged, against my learning to read, only served to inspire me with a desire and determination to learn. In learning to read, I owe almost as much to the bitter opposition of my master, as to the kindly aid of my mistress. I acknowledge the benefit of both.

[. . .]

I lived in Master Hugh's family about seven years. During this time, I succeeded in learning to read and write. In accomplishing this, I was compelled to resort to various stratagems. I had no regular teacher. My mistress, who had kindly commenced to instruct me, had, in compliance with the advice and direction of her husband, not only ceased to instruct, but had set her face against my being instructed by any one else. It is due, however, to my mistress to say of her, that she did not adopt this course of treatment immediately. She at first lacked the depravity indispensable to shutting me up in mental darkness. It was at least necessary for her to have some training in the exercise of irresponsible power, to make her equal to the task of treating me as though I were a brute.

My mistress was, as I have said, a kind and tender-hearted woman; and in the simplicity of her soul she commenced, when I first went to live with her, to treat me as she supposed one human being ought to treat another. In entering upon the duties of a slaveholder, she did not seem to perceive that I sustained to her the relation of a mere chattel, and that for her to treat me as a human being was not only wrong, but dangerously so. Slavery proved as injurious to her as it did to me. When I went there, she was a pious, warm, and tender-hearted woman. There was no sorrow or suffering for which she had not a tear. She had bread for the hungry, clothes for the naked, and comfort for every mourner that came within her reach. Slavery soon proved its ability to divest her of these heavenly qualities. Under its influence, the tender heart became stone, and the lamblike disposition gave way to one of tiger-like fierceness. The first step in her downward course was in her ceasing to instruct me. She now commenced to practise her husband's precepts. She finally became even more violent in her opposition than her husband himself. She was not satisfied with simply doing as well as he had commanded; she seemed anxious to do better. Nothing seemed to make her more angry than to see me with a newspaper. She seemed to think that here lay the danger. I have had her rush at me with a face made all up of fury, and snatch from me a newspaper, in a manner that fully revealed her apprehension. She was an apt woman; and a little experience soon demonstrated, to

115

her satisfaction, that education and slavery were incompatible with each other.

From this time I was most narrowly watched. If I was in a separate room any considerable length of time, I was sure to be suspected of having a book, and was at once called to give an account of myself. All this, however, was too late. The first step had been taken. Mistress, in teaching me the alphabet, had given me the *inch*, and no precaution could prevent me from taking the *ell*.

The plan which I adopted, and the one by which I was most successful, was that of making friends of all the little white boys whom I met in the street. As many of these as I could, I converted into teachers. With their kindly aid, obtained at different times and in different places, I finally succeeded in learning to read. When I was sent on errands, I always took my book with me, and by going one part of my errand quickly, I found time to get a lesson before my return. I used also to carry bread with me, enough of which was always in the house, and to which I was always welcome; for I was much better off in this regard than many of the poor white children in our neighborhood. This bread I used to bestow upon the hungry little urchins, who, in return, would give me that more valuable bread of knowledge. I am strongly tempted to give the names of two or three of those little boys, as a testimonial of the gratitude and affection I bear them; but prudence forbids; – not that it would injure me, but it might embarrass them; for it is almost an unpardonable offence to teach slaves to read in this Christian country. It is enough to say of the dear little fellows, that they lived on Philpot Street, very near Durgin and Bailey's ship-yard. I used to talk this matter of slavery over with them. I would sometimes say to them, I wished I could be as free as they would be when they got to be men. 'You will be free as soon as you are twenty-one, *but I am a slave for life!* Have not I as good a right to be free as you have?' These words used to trouble them; they would express for me the liveliest sympathy, and console me with the hope that something would occur by which I might be free.

Frederick Douglass (1817–1895)

Ideas for discussion

- Why do you think Douglass's new mistress (Mrs Auld) treated her slaves so unusually at first? What makes her change?

- Why do you think that Mr Auld believes an educated slave would be dangerous?

- Douglass implies that slavery had an evil effect on whites as well as blacks. Why do you think this might be?

- Do you think that Mr and Mrs Auld are evil people?

Suggestions for writing

Douglass and the other slaves were denied education. They were prevented from learning to read and, if they learned, were forbidden books. Can you imagine what it might be like to live in such a world?

Imagine a future society in which certain people are forced to be illiterate slaves. Any slave caught reading would be severely punished, possibly even executed. However, there is an underground movement teaching slaves to read. Write a story set in such a society.

(There are three famous modern novels that deal with this kind of idea: *Brave New World* by Aldous Huxley, *1984* by George Orwell and *Farenheit 541* by Ray Bradbury.)

● Who Am I? ●

James Weldon Johnson was one of the most influential American black activists of his time. In 1916 he became the first black executive secretary of the National Association for the Advancement of Colored People and succeeded in making lynching illegal.

By 1912, when *The Autobiography of an Ex-colored Man* was published, slavery had been abolished in America, but black people were still far from free.

James Weldon Johnson's book was one of the first to present a frank picture of being black in America. Despite its title, it is the fictional account of a man of mixed race growing up in Connecticut and then exploring the segregated southern states. The hero refers to himself as an 'ex-colored man' because he is able to pass himself off as a white man and at the end of the novel he chooses to live as one.

The following episode takes place when he is nine and has recently started to attend school. It is only then that he begins to learn who he is.

There were some black and brown boys and girls in the school, and several of them were in my class. One of the boys strongly attracted my attention from the first day I saw him. His face was as black as night, but shone as though it were polished; he had sparkling eyes, and when he opened his mouth, he displayed glistening white teeth. It struck me at once as appropriate to call him 'Shiny Face,' or 'Shiny Eyes,' or 'Shiny Teeth,' and I spoke of him often by one of these names to the other boys. These terms were finally merged into 'Shiny', and to that name he answered good-naturedly during the balance of his public school days.

'Shiny' was considered without question to be the best speller, the best reader, the best penman – in a word, the best scholar, in the class. He was very quick to catch anything, but, nevertheless, studied hard; thus he possessed two powers very rarely combined in one boy. I saw him year after year, on up into the high school, win the majority of the prizes for punctuality, deportment, essay writing, and declamation. Yet it did not take me long to discover that, in spite of his standing as a scholar, he was in some way looked down upon.

The other black boys and girls were still more looked down upon. Some of the boys often spoke of them as 'niggers.'

Sometimes on the way home from school a crowd would walk behind them repeating:

> '*Nigger, nigger, never die,*
> *Black face and shiny eye.*'

On one such afternoon one of the black boys turned suddenly on his tormentors and hurled a slate; it struck one of the white boys in the mouth, cutting a slight gash in his lip. At sight of the blood the boy who had thrown the slate ran, and his companions quickly followed. We ran after them pelting them with stones until they separated in several directions. I was very much wrought up over the affair, and went home and told my mother how one of the 'niggers' had struck a boy with a slate. I shall never forget how she turned on me. 'Don't you ever use that word again,' she said, 'and don't you ever bother the colored children at school. You ought to be ashamed of yourself.' I did hang my head in shame, not because she had convinced me that I had done wrong, but because I was hurt by the first sharp word she had ever given me.

My school days ran along very pleasantly. I stood well in my studies, not always so well with regard to my behavior. I was never guilty of any serious misconduct, but my love of fun sometimes got me into trouble. I remember, however, that my sense of humor was so sly that most of the trouble usually fell on the head of the other fellow. My ability to play on the piano at school exercises was looked upon as little short of marvelous in a boy of my age. I was not chummy with many of my mates, but, on the whole, was about as popular as it is good for a boy to be.

One day near the end of my second term at school the principal came into our room and, after talking to the teacher, for some reason said: 'I wish all of the white scholars to stand for a moment.' I rose with the others. The teacher looked at me and, calling my name, said. 'You sit down for the present, and rise with the others.' I did not quite understand her, and questioned: 'Ma'm? She repeated, with a softer tone in her voice: 'You sit down now, and rise with the others.' I sad down dazed. I saw and heard nothing. When the others were asked to rise, I did not know it. When school was dismissed, I went out in a kind of stupor. A few of the white boys jeered me, saying: 'Oh, you're a nigger too.' I heard some black children say: 'We knew he was colored.' 'Shiny' said to them: 'Come along, don't tease him,' and thereby won my undying gratitude.

All of these slaves were owned by one man, James Hopkinson.

I hurried on as fast as I could, and had gone some distance before I perceived that 'Red Head' was walking by my side. After a while he said to me: 'Le' me carry your books.' I gave him my strap without being able to answer. When we got to my gate, he said as he handed me my books: 'Say, you know my big red agate? I can't shoot with it any more. I'm going to bring it to school for you tomorrow.' I took my books and ran into the house. As I passed through the hallway, I saw that my mother was busy with one of her customers; I rushed up into my own little room, shut the door, and went quickly to where my looking-glass hung on the wall. For an instant I was afraid to look, but when I did, I looked long and earnestly. I had often heard people say to my mother: 'What a pretty boy you have!' I was accustomed to hear remarks about my beauty; but now, for the first time, I became conscious of it and recognized it. I noticed the ivory whiteness of my skin, the beauty of my mouth, the size and liquid darkness of my eyes, and how the long, black lashes that fringed and shaded them produced an effect that was strangely fascinating even to me. I noticed the softness and glossiness of my dark hair that fell in waves over my temples, making my forehead appear whiter than it really was. How long I stood there gazing at my image I do not know. When I came out and reached the head of the stairs, I heard the lady who had been with my mother going out. I ran downstairs and rushed to where my mother was sitting, with a piece of work in her hands. I buried my head in her lap and blurted out: 'Mother, mother, tell me, am I a nigger?' I could not see her face, but I knew the piece of work dropped to the floor and I felt her hands on my head. I looked up into her face and repeated: 'Tell me, mother, am I a nigger?' There were tears in her eyes and I could see that she was suffering for me. And then it was that I looked at her critically for the first time. I had thought of her in a childish way only as the most beautiful woman in the world; now I looked at her searching for defects. I could see that her skin was almost brown, that her hair was not so soft as mine, and that she did differ in some way from the other ladies who came to the house; yet, even so, I could see that she was very beautiful, more beautiful than any of them. She must have felt that I was examining her, for she hid her face in my hair and said with difficulty: 'No, my darling, you are not a nigger.' She went on: 'You are as good as anybody; if anyone calls you a nigger, don't notice them.' But the more she talked, the less was I reassured, and I stopped her by asking: 'Well, mother, am I white? Are you white?' She answered tremblingly: 'No, I am not white, but you – your father is one the greatest men in the country – the best blood of the South is in you –' This suddenly opened up in my heart a fresh chasm of misgiving and fear, and I almost fiercely demanded: 'Who is my father? Where is he?' She stroked my hair and said: 'I'll tell you about him some day.' I sobbed: 'I want to know now.' She answered: 'No, not now.'

Perhaps it had to be done, but I have never forgiven the woman who did it so cruelly. It may be that she never knew that she gave me a sword-thrust that day in school which was years in healing.

James Weldon Johnson (1871–1938)

Ideas for discussion

- Why do you think that Johnson chose to make his hero of mixed race rather than a black man like himself?

- The character has to go back to school the next day. How do you think he might feel and act now that he knows his racial identity?

- Later in the book, Johnson's hero (he is never named) says that, after that experience at school, his life changes – that every black person 'is forced to take his outlook on all things, not from the viewpoint of a citizen, or a man, or even a human being, but from the viewpoint of a *colored* man.' Do you think that this is still true in modern Britain?

- At the end of the book, the hero is happily married to a white woman and describes himself with a tinge of regret as 'an ordinarily successful white man'. Why do you think he chose to live as a white man? And why do you think he might regret his decision?

Suggestions for writing

How might the boy's relationship with 'Shiny' develop, now that he knows that he is 'colored'?

Write an episode from the story in which the two boys discuss their feelings about the attitudes to race that surround them and the way that they are treated at school.

Women speak out

Today, even the most highly educated person could probably not name more than six pre-twentieth century women writers as, for most of the history of English literature, women have been discouraged from publishing their writing. The reasons for this are very complex but certainly have their roots in the fact that very few women were allowed the kind of education that men have always taken for granted. Alongside this is the undeniable fact that until this century women were prevented from taking part in the wider world and were restricted to the home.

FOR BETTER, FOR WORSE.

Mistress. "I'M SORRY YOU WANT TO LEAVE, ELLIS. ARE YOU GOING TO BETTER YOURSELF?"
Maid. "No, M'M; I'M GOING TO GET MARRIED."

Despite these obvious handicaps, women have always written, even if they have not always been published, and it is only now that publishers are beginning to discover the wealth of pre-twentieth century women's writing.

This section of the unit comprises three poems together with two extracts from the first feminist manifesto.

In 1699, Mr Sprint, a Nonconformist minister, published a sermon criticising women's weak moral nature and advocating absolute obedience to their husbands. Lady Mary Chudleigh, a highly educated woman, wasted no time and published this spirited defence in 1701. The whole poem is rather long and is spoken by four characters: a tyrannical husband, a misogynistic parson, a dim and chivalrous man, and Melissa who tells them all a thing or two. 'To the Ladies' speaks for itself.

from *The Ladies Defence*
Or, the Bride-Woman's Counsellor Answered

Melissa: Unhappy they, who by their duty led,
Are made the partners of a hated bed;
And by their father's avarice or pride,
To empty fops, or nauseous clowns are tied;
Or else constrained to give up all their charms
Into an old ill-humoured husband's arms,
Who hugs his bags, and never was inclined
To be to aught besides his money kind,
Who's always positive in what is ill,
And still a slave to his imperious will:
Averse to any thing he thinks will please,
Still stick and still in love with his disease:
With fears, with discontent, with envy curst,
To all uneasy, and himself the worst:
A spiteful censor of the present age,
Or dully jesting, or deformed with rage [. . .]
    'Tis hard we should be by the men despised,
Yet kept from knowing what would make us prized:
Debarred from knowledge, banished from the schools,
And with the utmost industry bred fools.
Laughed out of reason, jested out of sense,
And nothing left but native innocence:
Then told we are incapable of wit,
And only for the meanest drudgeries fit:
Made slaves to serve their luxury and pride,
And with innumerable hardships tried,
Till pitying Heav'n release us from our pain [. . .]

They think, if we our thoughts can but express,
And know but how to work, to dance and dress,
It is enough, as much as we should mind,
As if we were for nothing else designed,
But made, like puppets, to divert mankind.
O that my sex would all such toys despise;
And only study to be good, and wise [. . .]
    Through all the labyrinth of learning go,
And grow more humble, as they more do know.
By doing this, they will respect procure,
Silence the men, and lasting fame secure;
And to themselves the best companions prove,
And neither fear their malice, nor desire their love.

To the Ladies

Wife and servant are the same,
But only differ in the name:
For when that fatal knot is tied,
When she the word *Obey* has said,
And man by law supreme has made,
Then all that's kind is laid aside,
And nothing left but state and pride.
Fierce as an eastern prince he grows,
And all his innate rigour shows:
Then but to look, to laugh, or speak,
Will the nuptial contract break.
Like mutes, she signs alone must make,
And never any freedom take.
But still be governed by a nod,
And fear her husband as her god:
Him still must serve, him still obey,
And nothing act, and nothing say,
But what her haughty lord thinks fit
Who, with the power, has all the wit.
Then shun, oh! shun that wretched state,
And all the fawning flatt'rers hate.
Value yourselves, and men despise:
You must be proud, if you'll be wise.

Lady Mary Chudleigh (1656–1710)

The Wish, By a Young Lady

I ask not wit, nor beauty do I crave,
Nor wealth, nor pompous titles wish to have;
But since, 'tis doomed through all degrees of life,
Whether a daughter, sister, or a wife;
That females should the stronger males obey,
And yield implicit to their lordly sway;
Since this, I say, is ev'ry woman's fate,
Give me a mind to suit my slavish state.

Laetitia Pilkington (c.1712–1750)

Mary Collier worked as an agricultural labourer and this extract from her poem, 'The Woman's Labour', paints a vivid picture of the realities of eighteenth-century labouring life. It was written in reply to a poem, 'The Thresher's Labour' by Stephen Duck, which accused labourers of laziness.

from *The Woman's Labour*

For my own part, I many a summer's day
Have spent in throwing, turning, making hay;
But ne'er could see, what you have lately found,
Our wages paid for sitting on the ground.
'Tis true, that when our morning's work is done,
And all our grass exposed unto the sun,
While that his scorching beams do on it shine,
As well as you we have time to dine:
I hope, that since we freely toil and sweat
To earn our bread, you'll give us time to eat;
That over, soon we must get up again,
And nimbly turn our hay upon the plain;
Nay, rake and row it in, the case is clear,
Or how should cocks in equal rows appear?
But if you'd have what you have wrote believed,
I find, that you to hear us talk are grieved:
In this, I hope you do not speak your mind,
For none but Turks, that ever I could find,
Have mutes to serve them, or did e'er deny
Their slaves at work, to chat it merrily.
Since you have liberty to speak your mind,
And are to talk, as well as we, inclined,
Why should you thus repine, because that we,
Like you, enjoy that pleasing liberty?
What! would you lord it quite, and take away
The only privilege our sex enjoy?

When ev'ning does approach, we homeward hie
And our domestic toils incessant ply:
Against your coming home prepare to get
Our work all done, our house in order set;
Bacon and dumpling in the pot we boil,
Our beds we make, our swine we feed the while;
Then wait at door to see you coming home,

And set the table out against you come.
Early next morning we on you attend,
Our children dress and feed, their clothes we mend;
And in the field our daily task renew,
Soon as the rising sun has dried the dew.

When harvest comes, into the field we go,
And help to reap the wheat as well as you;
Or else we go the ears of corn to glean,
No labour scorning, be it e'er so mean;
But in the work we freely bear a part,
And what we can, perform with all our heart.
To get a living we so willing are,
Our tender babes unto the field we bear,
And wrap them in our clothes to keep them warm,
While round about we gather in the corn;
And often unto them our course do bend,
To keep them safe, that nothing them offend;
Our children that are able bear a share
In gleaning corn, such is our frugal care.
When night comes on, unto our home we go,
Our corn we carry, and our infant too,
Weary indeed! but 'tis not worth our while
Once to complain, or rest at ev'ry stile;
We must make haste, for when we home are come,
We find again our work but just begun;
So many things for our attendance call,
Had we ten hands, we could employ them all.
Our children put to bed, with greatest care
We all things for your coming home prepare:
You sup, and go to bed without delay,
And rest yourselves till the ensuing day;
While we, alas! but little sleep can have,
Because our froward children cry and rave;
Yet, without fail, soon as day-light doth spring,
We in the field again our work begin,
And there, with all our strength, our toil renew,
Till Titan's golden rays have dried the dew;
Then home we go unto our children dear,
Dress, feed, and bring them to the field with care.
Were this your case, you justly might complain
That day or night you are secure from pain;
Those mightly troubles which perplex your mind

(Thistles before, and females come behind)
Would vanish soon, and quickly disappear,
Were you, like us, encumbered thus with care.
What you would have of us we do not know:
We oft take up the corn that you do mow,
We cut the peas, and always ready are
In every work to take our proper share;
And from the time that harvest doth begin,
Until the corn be cut and carried in,
Our toil and labour's daily so extreme,
That we have hardly ever time to dream.

Mary Collier (dates unknown)

• An Adorable Prison •

When Mary Wollstonecraft published her 'Vindication of The Rights of Woman' in 1792, she was described as 'a hyena in petticoats'. However, her work can now be seen as the precursor of the modern feminist movement. In these extracts she bemoans the fact that men's excessive gentility and protectiveness towards women add to their oppression.

Most men are sometimes obliged to bear with bodily incon-veniences, and to endure, occasionally, the inclemency of the elements; but genteel women are, literally speaking, slaves to their bodies, and glory in their subjection.

I once knew a weak woman of fashion, who was more than commonly proud of her delicacy and sensibility. She thought a distinguishing taste and puny appetite the height of all human perfection, and acted accordingly. I have seen this weak sophisti-cated being neglect all the duties of life, yet recline with self-complacency on a sofa, and boast of her want of appetite as a proof of delicacy that extended to, or, perhaps, arose from, her exquisite sensibility; for it is difficult to render intelligible such ridiculous jargon. Yet, at the moment, I have seen her insult a worthy old gentlewoman, whom unexpected misfortunes had made dependent on her ostentatious bounty, and who, in better days, had claims on her gratitude. Is it possible that a human creature could have become such a weak and depraved being, if, like Sybarites, dissolved in luxury, everything like virtue had not been worn away, or never impressed by precept, a poor substitute, it is true, for cultivation of mind, though it serves as a fence against vice?

Such a woman is not a more irrational monster than some of the Roman emperors, who were depraved by lawless power. Yet, since kings have been more under the restraint of law, and the curb, however weak, of honour, the records of history are not filled with such unnatural instances of folly and cruelty, nor does the despotism that kills virtue and genius in the bud, hover over Europe with that destructive blast which desolates Turkey, and renders men, as well as the soil, unfruitful.

Women are everywhere in this deplorable state; for, in order to preserve their innocence, as ignorance is courteously termed, truth is hidden from them, and they are made to assume an artificial character before their faculties have acquired any strength. Taught from their infancy that beauty is woman's sceptre, the mind shapes itself to the body, and roaming round its gilt cage, only seeks to adore its prison. Men have various employments and pursuits which engage their attention, and give a character to the opening mind; but women, confined to one, and having their thoughts constantly directed to most insignificant part of themselves, seldom extend their views beyond the triumph of the hour. But were their understanding once emancipated from the slavery to which the pride and sensuality of man and their short-sighted desire, like that of dominion in tyrants, of present sway, has subjected them, we should probably read of their weaknesses with surprise.

[...]

I lament that women are systematically degraded by receiving the trivial attentions which men think it manly to pay to the sex, when in fact, they are insultingly supporting their own superiority. It is not condescension to bow to an inferior. So ludicrous, in fact, do these ceremonies appear to me that I scarcely am able to govern my muscles when I see a man start with eager and serious solicitude to lift a handkerchief or shut a door, when the *lady* could have done it herself, had she only moved a pace or two.

A wild wish has just flown from my heart to my head, and I will not stifle it, though it may excite a horse-laugh. I do earnestly wish to see the distinction of sex confounded in society, unless where love animates the behaviour. For this distinction is, I am firmly persuaded, the foundation of the weakness of character ascribed to woman; is the cause why the understanding is neglected, whilst accomplishments are acquired with sedulous care; and the same cause accounts for their preferring the graceful before the heroic virtues.

Mankind, including every description, wish to be loved and respected by *something*, and the common herd will always take the nearest road to the completion of their wishes. The respect paid to wealth and beauty is the most certain and unequivocal, and, of course, will always attract the vulgar eye of common minds. Abilities and virtues are absolutely necessary to raise men from the middle rank of life into notice, and the natural consequence is notorious – the middle rank contains most virtue and abilities. Men have thus, in one station at least, an opportunity of exerting themselves with dignity, and of rising by the exertions which really improve a rational creature; but the whole female sex are, till their character is formed, in the same condition as the rich, for they are born – I now speak of a state of civilization – with certain sexual privileges; and whilst they are gratuitously granted them, few will ever think of works of supererogation to obtain the esteem of a small number of superior people.

When do we hear of women who, starting out of obscurity, boldly claim respect on account of their great abilities or daring virtues? Where are they to be found?

Mary Wollstonecraft (1759–1797)

Suffragettes being arrested near Buckingham Palace in 1914.

• Mrs Pankhurst's address to the jury •

Emmeline Pankhurst was one of the founders of the Suffragette Movement, dedicated to winning women the right to vote in the early part of this century. She also believed in civil disobedience and, along with many other women was arrested for 'malicious incitement' during a demonstration. What follows is her address to the jury (a jury made up of men because women were not allowed to sit on juries).

'Over one thousand women have gone to prison in the course of this agitation, have suffered their imprisonment, have come out of prison injured in health, weakened in body, but not in spirit. I come to stand my trial from the bedside of one of my daughters, who has come out of Holloway Prison, sent there for two months' hard labour for participating with four other people in breaking a small pane of glass. She has hunger-struck in prison. She submitted herself for more than five weeks to the horrible ordeal of feeding by force, and she has come out of prison having lost nearly two stone in weight. She is so weak that she cannot get out of her bed. And I say to you, gentlemen, that is the kind of punishment you are inflicting upon me or any other woman who may be brought before you. I ask you if you are prepared to send an incalculable number of women to prison – I speak to you as representing others in the same position – if you are prepared to go on doing that kind of thing indefinitely, because that is what is going to happen. There is absolutely no doubt about it. I think you have seen enough even in this present case to convince you that we are not women who are notoriety hunters. We could get that, heaven knows, much more cheaply if we sought it. We are women, rightly or wrongly, convinced that this is the only way in which we can win power to alter what for us are intolerable conditions, absolutely intolerable conditions. A London clergyman only the other day said that 60 per cent. of the married women in his parish were breadwinners, supporting their husbands as well as their children. When you think of the wages women earn, when you think of what this means to the future of the children of this country, I ask you to take this question very, very seriously. Only this morning I have had information brought to me which could be supported by sworn affidavits, that there is in this country, in this very city of London of ours, a regulated traffic, not only in women of full age, but in little children; that they are being purchased, that they are being entrapped, and that they are being trained to minister to the vicious pleasures of persons who ought to know better in their positions of life.

'Well, these are the things that have made us women determined to go on, determined to face everything, determined to see this thing out to the end, let it cost us what it may. And if you convict me, gentlemen, if you find me guilty, I tell you quite honestly and quite frankly, that whether the sentence is a long sentence, whether the sentence is a short sentence, I shall not submit to it. I shall, the moment I leave this court, if I am sent to prison, whether to penal servitude or to the lighter form of imprisonment – because I am not sufficiently versed in the law to know what his lordship may decide; but whatever my sentence is, from the moment I leave this court I shall quite deliberately refuse to eat food – I shall join the women who are already in Holloway on the hunger strike. I shall come out of prison, dead or alive, at the earliest possible moment; and once out again, as soon as I am physically fit I shall enter into this fight again. Life is very dear to all of us. I am not seeking, as was said by the Home Secretary, to commit suicide. I do not want to commit suicide. I want to see the women of this country enfranchised, and I want to live until that is done. Those are the feelings by which we are animated. We offer ourselves as sacrifices, just as your forefathers did in the past, in this cause, and I would ask you all to put this question to yourselves: – Have you the right, as human beings, to condemn another human being to death – because that is what it amounts to? Can you throw the first stone? Have you the right to judge women?

'You have not the right in human justice, not the right by the constitution of this country, if rightly interpreted, to judge me, because you are not my peers. You know, every one of you, that I should not be standing here, that I should not break one single law – if I had the rights that you possess, if I had a share in electing those who make the laws I have to obey; if I had a voice in controlling the taxes I am called upon to pay, I should not be standing here. And I say to you it is a very serious state of things. I say to you, my lord, it is a very serious situation, that women of upright life, women who have devoted the best of their years to the public weal, that women who are engaged in trying to undo some of the terrible mistakes that men in their government of the country have made, because after all, in the last resort, men are responsible for the present state of affairs – I put it to you that it is a very serious situation. You are not accustomed to deal

Emmeline and Christabel Pankhurst in 1909.

with people like me in the ordinary discharge of your duties; but you are called upon to deal with people who break the law from selfish motives. I break the law from no selfish motive. I have no personal end to serve, neither have any of the other women who have gone through this court during the past few weeks, like sheep to the slaughter. Not one of these women would, if women were free, be law-breakers. They are women who seriously believe that this hard path that they are treading is the only path to their enfranchisement. They seriously believe that the welfare of humanity demands this sacrifice; they believe that the horrible evils which are ravaging our civilisation will never be removed until women get the vote. They know that the very fount of life is being poisoned; they know that homes are being destroyed; that because of bad education, because of the unequal standard of morals, even the mothers and children are destroyed by one of the vilest and most horrible diseases that ravage humanity.

'There is only one way to put a stop to this agitation; there is only one way to break down this agitation. It is not by deporting us, it is not by locking us up in gaol; it is by doing us justice. And so I appeal to you gentlemen, in this case of mine, to give a verdict, not only on my case, but upon the whole of this agitation. I ask you to find me not guilty of malicious incitement to a breach of the law.

'These are my last words. My incitement is not malicious. If I had power to deal with these things, I would be in absolute obedience to the law. I would say to women, "You have a constitutional means of getting redress for your grievances; use your votes, convince your fellow-voters of the righteousness of your demands. That is the way to obtain justice." I am not guilty of malicious incitement, and I appeal to you, for the welfare of the country, for the welfare of the race, to return a verdict of not guilty in this case that you are called upon to try.'

Emmeline Pankhurst (1858–1928)

Ideas for discussion

■ Read the poems and extracts carefully, and make a list of the things that the writers feel are wrong with the way society treats them.

When you have completed the list, group the ideas under headings (for example, Education or Work).

Using your list, devise between five and ten changes that you feel the writers might call for to improve women's lives. Make sure that you come up with at least one change for each heading. How would they like the education system to change, for instance?

■ Do you feel that women's role in society has changed since the eighteenth century, as presented by these poems and extracts? If so, in what ways? Have all the changes that these women called for taken place?

■ Pankhurst suggests action rather than talk as a way of changing society. How do you feel about the idea of civil disobedience? Would you be prepared to take action of this sort?

Can you think of any modern movements which have attempted to change things in this way? How successful have they been?

Suggestions for writing

1 Write about the way you felt as a modern young woman or man reading these poems and extracts. What picture of women's lives did you gain from your reading, and how does it compare with women's lives today?

2 Write a modern version of 'The Womans Labour' in the form of a piece of creative writing entitled 'Scenes from the Lives of Twentieth Century Women'. It should consist of three or four scenes from the lives of different kinds of women who, in your view, represent the condition of contemporary women. You could, for instance, write about a school student, a young doctor and a shop assistant. Try to contrast the lives as much as possible, but you may feel that all your women have some experiences in common.

3 Imagine that you were able to see into the jury room during the jury's deliberations on Mrs. Pankhurst's case. Write a version of the discussion that might have taken place. Remember that she does not deny the charge but has explained the reasons for her actions.

4 Is there anything that you believe in so strongly that you would be prepared to go to prison for it? Write about it in such a way as to persuade others to join you in your action.

Or

Perhaps you feel that breaking the law can never be right. In which case explain the reasons for your belief in an essay.

Rosa Parks was arrested in 1955 for refusing to give up her bus seat to a white man. Her arrest led to the Alabama bus boycott which, eventually, resulted in the desegregation of public transport.
This photograph shows Rosa Parks on the first day of desegregation.

unit 5

Time

Time has always fascinated writers. It is a great mystery — we are forced to live in it but we do not understand what time is or how it works.

This unit consists of five poems and two pieces of prose that explore the nature of time and the way it affects our attitudes to the world.

Before you read on, here are some ideas for discussion that will help you to get the most out of your reading.

Discuss the following statements:

- Time destroys.

- Some things remain unchanged by time.

- We cannot escape time.

- Certain events seem to exist outside time.

Now read these poems and prose pieces that deal with the questions that will have arisen from your discussion.

To Daffodils

Fair Daffodils, we weep to see
    You hast away so soon
As yet the early-rising Sun
      Has not attain'd his noon.
        Stay, stay,
    Until the hasting day
      Has run
    But to the even-song;
And, having pray'd together, we
    Will go with you along.

We have short time to stay, as you
    We have as short a Spring;
As quick a growth to meet decay
    As you, or any thing.
      We die,
    As your hours do, and dry
      Away
    Like to the Summer's rain;
Or as the pearls of morning's dew
    Ne'er to be found again.

Robert Herrick (1591–1674)

Time and Love

When I have seen by Time's fell hand defaced
The rich proud cost of out-worn buried age;
When sometime lofty towers I see down-razed,
And brass eternal slave to mortal rage;

When I have seen the hungry ocean gain
Advantage on the kingdom of the shore,
And the firm soil win of the watery main,
Increasing store with loss, and loss with store;

When I have seen such interchange of state,
Or state itself confounded to decay,
Ruin hath taught me thus to ruminate –
That Time will come and take my Love away:

– This thought is as a death, which cannot choose
But weep to have that which it fears to lose.

William Shakespeare (1564–1616)

Get Drunk!

One should always be drunk. That's all that matters; that's our one imperative need. So as not to feel Time's horrible burden that breaks your shoulders and bows you down, you must get drunk without ceasing.

But what with? With wine, with poetry, or with virtue, as you choose. But get drunk.

And if, at some time, on the steps of a palace, in the green grass of a ditch, in the bleak solitude of your room, you are waking up when drunkenness has already abated, ask the wind, the wave, a star, the clock, all that which flees, all that which groans, all that which rolls, all that which sings, all that which speaks, ask them what time it is; and the wind, the wave, the star, the bird, the clock will reply: 'It is time to get drunk! So that you may not be the martyred slaves of Time, get drunk; get drunk, and never pause for rest! With wine, with poetry, or with virtue, as you choose!'

Charles Baudelaire (1821–1867) translated by
Michael Hamburger (1924–)

In Time of 'The Breaking of Nations'

I

Only a man harrowing clods
　In a slow silent walk
With an old horse that stumbles and nods
　Half asleep as they stalk.

II

Only thin smoke without flame
　From the heaps of couch-grass;
Yet this will go onward the same
　Though Dynasties pass.

III

Yonder a maid and her wight
　Come whispering by:
War's annals will cloud into night
　Ere their story die.

Thomas Hardy (1840–1928)

Ozymandias of Egypt

I met a traveller from an antique land
Who said: Two vast and trunkless legs of stone
Stand in the desert. Near them on the sand
Half sunk, a shatter'd visage lies, whose frown
And wrinkled lip and sneer of cold command
Tell that its sculptor well those passions read
Which yet survive, stamp'd on these lifeless things,
The hand that mock'd them and the heart that fed;
And on the pedestal these words appear:
'My name is Ozymandias, king of kings:
Look on my works, ye Mighty, and despair!'
Nothing beside remains. Round the decay
Of that colossal wreck, boundless and bare,
The lone and level sands stretch far away.

Percy Bysshe Shelley (1792–1822)

The Sphynx

And near the Pyramids, more wondrous and more awful than all else in the land of Egypt, there sits the lonely Sphynx. Comely the creature is, but the comeliness is not of this world: the once worshipped beast is a deformity and a monster to this generation; and yet you can see that those lips, so thick and heavy, were fashioned according to some ancient mould of beauty – some mould of beauty now forgotten – forgotten because that Greece drew forth Cytherea* from the flashing foam of the Ægean, and in her image created new forms of beauty, and made it a law among men that the short and proudly-wreathed lip should stand for the sign and the main condition of loveliness through all generations to come. Yet still there lives on the race of those who were beautiful in the fashion of the elder world; and Christian girls of Coptic blood will look on you with the sad, serious gaze, and kiss your charitable hand with the big pouting lips of the very Sphynx.

Laugh and mock if you will at the worship of stone idols; but mark ye this, ye breakers of images, that in one regard, the stone idol bears awful semblance of Deity – unchangefulness in the midst of change – the same seeming will and intent for ever and ever inexorable! Upon ancient dynasties of Ethiopian and Egyptian kings – upon Greek and Roman, upon Arab and Ottoman conquerors – upon Napoleon dreaming of an Eastern empire – upon battle and pestilence – upon the ceaseless misery of the Egyptian race – upon keen-eyed travellers – Herodotus yesterday, and Warburton to-day – upon all and more this unworldly Sphynx has watched, and watched like a Providence with the same earnest eyes, and the same sad, tranquil mien. And we, we shall die, and Islam will whither away; and the Englishman, straining far over to hold his loved India, will plant a firm foot on the banks of the Nile and sit in the seats of the Faithful, and still that sleepless rock will lie watching and watching the works of the new busy race, with those same sad earnest eyes, and the same tranquil mien everlasting. You dare not mock at the Sphynx.

Alexander Kinglake (1809–1891)

Cytherea refers to Aphrodite, the Greek goddess of love and beauty, who was born out of the sea and was reputed to have a shrine on the island of Cythera. Her features, as immortalised in statues like the Venus de Milo, became the model for both male and female beauty.

'There came a Wind like a Bugle'

There came a Wind like a Bugle –
It quivered through the Grass
And a Green Chill upon the Heat
So ominous did pass
We barred the Windows and the Doors
As from an Emerald Ghost –
The Doom's electric Moccasin
That very instant passed –
On a strange Mob of panting Trees
And Fences fled away
And Rivers where the Houses ran
Those looked that lived – that Day –
The Bell within the steeple wild
The flying tidings told –
How much can come
And much can go,
And yet abide the World!

Emily Dickinson (1830–1886)

Ideas for discussion

- What is each writer saying about time? Discuss the ideas that the writers use to put forward their views of time.

- Is it possible, according to these writers, to escape from the effects of time? If so, what is it that escapes, and how?

Suggestions for writing

1 Write an essay in which you discuss these prose pieces and peoms, and explore the ways in which each of them examines the nature of time. You may want to concentrate on two or three of them in detail.

2 Write a series of poems or pieces of descriptive prose which examine the various ways in which time is experienced. Here are some ideas to help you:

- A student daydreams through the last lesson of the day.

- The thoughts of a small child lying in bed the night before a birthday or Christmas.

- A car crash victim describes the moment of impact imprinted on his or her mind as if time had stood still.

- An old woman or man describes her or his childhood as if it were yesterday.

- Someone from a thousand years into the future is walking through what used to be the site of your school. He or she finds an old exercise book (yours?).

- The thoughts of someone walking around an old deserted house.

- Someone goes up into his or her attic and finds a box full of old love letters.